Asking For Wonder

Resources For Creative
Worship And Preaching

Elaine M. Ward

CSS Publishing Company, Inc., Lima, Ohio

Scripture quotations are from the *New Revised Standard Version of the Bible*, copyright 1989 by the Division of Christian Education of the National Council of the Churches of Christ in the USA. Used by permission.

Library of Congress Cataloging-in-Publication Data

Ward, Elaine M.
  Asking for wonder : resources for creative worship and preaching / Elaine M. Ward.
      p.   cm.
  Includes bibliographical references.
  ISBN 0-7880-1061-1 (pbk.)
  1. Public worship. 2. Preaching.   I. Title.
BV15.W35   1997
264—dc21   96-53588
                                                                                 CIP

This book is available in the following formats, listed by ISBN:
      0-7880-1061-1   Book
      0-7880-1107-3   Mac
      0-7880-1108-1   IBM 3 1/2
      0-7880-1109-X   Sermon Prep

To Terry Dowdy,
friend, pastor, and
creative worship leader.

Table Of Contents

Introduction

"... And they were filled with wonder and amazement ..."
(Acts 3:10b).

I ask proof of Your existence,
God of heaven and earth,
Reveal to me Your word and presence.
Let me sense Your Spirit.

And the wind blew
A child laughed
A bird sang
A whisp of cloud floated by ...

I asked for wisdom, Lord,
    and you gave me wonder.

Wonder is the ability to be open to surprise and possibility. It is the source of gratitude, expectancy, and trust, the attitude of awareness of the holy, the quality of an authentic and abundant life. The response to wonder is worship.

Asking for Wonder, a gathering of resources for worship, is a call to beauty, celebration, and God: the possibilities of the present. When we cease to grow and risk, the Spirit becomes stagnant in our lives and in our words. It is a gathering of stories, prose and poetry, as calls to worship, prayers of confession, of praise, affirmations of faith, liturgies, scripture readings and benedictions.

These resources for worship, celebrating wonder in praise of God, the Creator of wonder, were written out of an awareness of the importance of the imagination to nourish and nurture the sensitivities of the human spirit that encourage us to celebrate a living faith that trusts the sublime Mystery who is our Creator and Lord.

We worship in order:

1. To experience the presence of God through sight, sound, silence, smell, taste, and hearing.

2. To respond to God by participating in the acts of worship: confession, affirmation, praise, thanksgiving, petition, and intercessory prayer, the sacraments of baptism and communion, and the hearing of the Scriptures.

3. To participate in the community of believers that heals, nourishes, and sustains, in order to form, feed, and transform one's personal and corporate faith.

4. To educate the young (new and growing Christians) in the love and presence of God, the church season, proclamation of the biblical story, the purpose and importance of worship, both traditional and contemporary, direction for living the faith today, the meaning and purpose of the sacraments of the Word and Table, and service in the world in an atmosphere of joy and celebration.

In worship we see visions, expect miracles, and ask for wonder.

Asking for wonder,
I smell the scent of incense in the sanctuary
And taste the bread and wine,
Seeing the old and young kneel in petition and praise.
While feeling their hands in the passing of Christ's peace,
I hear their voices blend with the angel's singing,
"Fear not, behold, I bring good news."

I ask for wonder,
As the pastor feeds us with God's word of grace,
Leading us in intercessory prayer,
Believing in, thus bringing in, God's reign
Here among us in this temple
And now upon the city street,
Transforming our warring weapons
Into words of comfort for those we meet,
Hungry for love, craving for hope,
As the blind for sight,
The powerless for freedom.

I ask for wonder,
And creeds and creation merge,
Nature and reason,
The wonder of existence and the questions of the heart,
That higher ignorance before the silence of Mystery.

I ask for wonder,
And see a gnarled tree,
A withered hand,
And wonder there are trees and hands and gifts of wonder.

Wonder is the poetry of praise and appreciation,
The language of thanksgiving,
Celebrating doubt and the seeking of knowledge,
To transform them into beauty, wisdom, and compassion.

I ask for wonder
To see the sacred in the everyday,
Beauty in the deformed,
And eternity here and now.

To wonder in the presence of God and the community of faith, the body of Christ, through the power of the Holy Spirit, is to worship. To wonder is to see with the heart.

1

Worship

Worship is an art: a painting or sculpture or drama that helps us see, a psalm, a hymn, a sermon that helps us hear, a sacrament we taste, a baptism we experience, a hand we touch in passing the peace of Christ, the wonder we smell because we are "the odor of God" in the sanctuary, the prayer we speak from the heart, and the word we receive from God.

Worship is a way for the community to speak and act out their identity, faith, and mission, their vision and their search for new vision. It is the people's work. It is not to be observed, but experienced. Those who are present participate. The Greek word for "liturgy" is an act of public service, the work of the people, not their entertainment. When worship, however, feels as drudgery, difficult work, it is time to reassess our worship. The "work of the people" means joyous participatory thanksgiving and praise of God.

Worship is the expression of praise, thanksgiving, confession in prayer and song, and the celebration of the word and sacraments that forms a people, passionately alive to the wonder, mystery, and glory of God's creation, into a community of faith, dependent on the tender mercies and grace of God. It gives formation and order to the community's affirmation of faith in the Source of all life and love, naming the world in a particular way, Jesus' way.

As work of the people, worship is designed to be relevant to our needs and integral to our faith. Tradition is "man" made. Thus, the image of "servanthood" is more appropriate to those who already have the power of authority, while marginalized or battered persons seeking power to exercise prefer the image of enabler or helper.

Worship with memory and imagination loosens the spirit and cares for the soul. "The use of the imagination is essential for the celebration of the sacraments and for the development of a sacramental understanding of all of life.[1]"

Our memories influence our sense of identity, give us our roots and meaning, our power to construct. We gather to remember what God has done through the stories of God's creating and liberating and sending forth. We gather around these core stories and reenact them in our worship. Ours is an embodied memory in the incarnation of Jesus Christ and in the community of faith as that body in the world.

A people worships and celebrates in and through its sacred stories and rites. Sacred stories tell of felt experience that cannot be expressed in literal description or explanation. "Performance of ritual that is not grounded in story is not really performance but only going through the motions."[2]

Without a memory for creation or a promise of restoration, there is no hope. Mere waiting is not enough. In the wasteland we ask, "Is this all?" The wilderness is barren. "The kingdom of God is within you."

Worship is the memory and celebration of our rituals of praise. Thomas Troeger writes of preparing a wedding sermon in the early hours before dawn, as he watches the moon in the crown of his great silver maple tree, like some heart pumping light down through the branches of the tree to its roots and up into his attic study. Then he reflects, "I feel part of a great capillary system that circulates truth from heaven to the earth through the city about me and the city of books on my desk and the couple I will marry and the congregation who, if they are moved to pray, will complete the cycle of spiritual energy through their act of praise."[3]

Liturgy enfleshes the rational text. It rescues meaning by reenacting the story. The real "teacher" is experience, and the story in the ritual transmits living energy and existential meaning.

In *Holy Power Human Pain,*[4] Dick Vieth closes with a powerfully compassionate story told by Yvonne Dilling of a liturgy celebrated in the refugee camp at La Virtud, Honduras, among the Salvadoran refugees. In the midst of the disruption, loss, illness, and danger, the liturgy began. "First they elaborated on their own suffering: three children a day have died of diarrhea and dehydration this past week," she wrote in her journal. "Many are sick with parasites, cough, headaches. 'We are strangers expelled from our land by foreign forces,' they said." "How is Jesus resurrected in us?" the catechist asked, and an old voice called out, "Only if we carry on with his work of building a better world where justice dwells and suffering is ended." There followed the liturgy of light, and in that light for fifteen minutes the valley was filled with voices recalling the names of children, mothers, fathers, priests, nuns ...

"But look, the dawn has come!" said the catechist. "The stone is rolling away, the tomb cannot hold him." At Christmas they again celebrated amid their misery and created a powerful Christmas celebration literally out of nothing. "Never have I experienced such a powerful Christmas celebration," wrote Dilling.

Vieth reflected, "They found their story in the biblical story, and that gave it a significance that no persecution could take away ... I cannot shake the conviction that this disheveled band, with all the foolishness of their hope, are stronger than all the powers arrayed against them. In the weird logic of my imagination, I see them as an incarnation of Jesus' words: 'In the world you have tribulation; but be of good cheer, I have overcome the world.' "

TO DO:

The following activities are suggested for engaging worshipers in participation:

1. Congregational feedback after the sermon or service of worship, such as a press conference with questions and answers.

2. Place in a conspicuous spot and call attention to a question or suggestion box for sermon topics to put on the pulpit agenda.

3. Engage in dialogue preaching.

4. Rearrange furniture so that the pulpit is among the people.

5. Some churches will have more than one service of worship because of the varying needs of their congregation and the need to reach the unchurched. When increasing options, you may wish to do it on an experimental basis for, say, two or three months and be sure to recognize whom you are trying to reach.

6. More and more churches are creating intergenerational gatherings for worship, celebration, and fellowship. This gathering can be held during the church worship hour, the church school hour, or in the evening during the week. Eating together is suggested as a way to say to one another, as the Hebrews did when they ate together, "You are my sister, my brother. I am responsible for you."

7. Worship is the church practicing its faith. Young children can be included, especially in the passing of peace. If this is new for your congregation, be patient. Adult attitudes change slowly. Until the congregation is comfortable with spontaneously passing the peace, give instructions, such as "Each person sitting on the center aisle seat of the pew shake the hand of the person next to you and say, 'The peace of Christ be with you' or simply 'Peace.' That person passes it on across the pew. Children are, of course, included."

8. Have you ever considered engaging your congregation in creating the worship service: call to worship, prayer of confession/absolution, affirmation of faith, hymns, offertory prayer, and sermon?

9. Some worship leaders recruit a team of volunteers, asking them to choose from the above and collect relevant sermon material on the texts to be preached. Ask them to bring their material the Sunday before it is to be used.

10. Individuals from the congregation stand up and voice their concerns, to be followed by the taking of Communion as a response to "What can we do?" We can be fed to feed, remembering Christ's presence here at the table and in the world.

11. On Thanksgiving invite the congregation to bring food gifts to present at the altar as they receive Communion.

12. Learn to make the sign of the cross. The sign of the cross in the Roman Catholic Church opens all liturgical celebrations. It is an appropriate sign for Protestants as well. The hand is placed on the forehead in the name of the Creator to whom we dedicate our knowledge, memory, imagination, and intellect: the mind. The hand is then lowered to the center of the chest and prayer continues in the name of Jesus Christ who loves and teaches us to love. The hand is next placed on the left shoulder in the name of the Holy Spirit who lives within and among us. Placing the hand on the left side we celebrate the creative, nurturing, emotional aspect of ourselves. We pray in the name of the Spirit as the hand is placed on the right side to celebrate the masculine aspect of our being, the logical, cognitive, forceful part of our spirit. As palms are placed together and fingers point to the sky, we remember that we are one, father/mother, son/daughter, united with all creation in the name of the Triune God.

13. Read and discuss Exodus 15:20; Psalm 30:11; 87:7; 149:3; 150:4; Ecclesiastes 3:4; 1 Samuel 21:11; 29:5; 2 Samuel 6:16; Jeremiah 31:4, 13; Matthew 11:17; and Luke 7:32.

14. Invite a dancer to enact the call to worship: Before the worship service began we waited in anticipation, when suddenly from the back of the church we heard bells ringing softly and approaching, as the dancer in a long black dress gracefully moved down the center aisle, shaking her bells, smiling at each of us individually as she proceeded to the altar. (I almost wrote "ascended," for she created that sense in her movement.) The lights in the sanctuary went on one by one until she moved up the stairs into the chancel area before the altar, welcoming us to worship. Expanding her arms in a wide, welcoming gesture, she smiled, and all of the lights filled the sanctuary with joy and peace, and we were in worship!

15. Engage in different kinds of movement in the worship service:
   a. Processional movement from one place to another.
   b. Proclamation movement, such as the call to worship or accompanying a story or scripture reading.
   c. Prayer dance through bodily prayers centered in the Doxology, the Lord's Prayer, the invocation by the congregation rather than one individual as above.
   d. Meditation without words, keeping in mind the sight impaired. When a worship leader announced that he/she would do a body prayer accompanied by native American sign-language, the blind person knew she was in trouble. A friend may move with that person and double the praise.
   e. Celebrative dance at the close of the service, such as standing around the outside aisle, holding hands, and moving to the music of the hymn "The Lord Of The Dance."
   Early church worship included the whole person: mind and body. An introduction to including the heart and the body is a slow and gradual process, an "education" leading the people out.

16. Sing "Spirit Of The Living God":
   a. Spirit of the living God, fall afresh on me,
   b. Spirit of the living God, fall afresh on me.
   c. Melt me, mold me, fill me, use me.
   d. Spirit of the living God, fall afresh on me.
   Body Prayer: Repeat the words of the hymn "Spirit Of The Living God" with movements:
   a. Stand, reach up; on word "living," stretch higher.
   b. Repeat.
   c. Melt me (shake hands descending); mold me (as potter molding clay); fill me (arms in front, hands toward body); use me (stretch arms forward).
   d. Repeat line b.

17. Pray in silence with an awareness of your bodily sensations: feet on floor, knee against knee, thighs on chair, hand against hand, back against chair, clothes on shoulders. Move from one part of the body to the other continuously. As you instruct the group, repeat the words aloud until quiet centering occurs.

18. Using your body, even though standing with arms limp at the sides, or raising hands above head, or stretching arms horizontally, and saying the words, "My God, I offer myself to you," can cause feelings of vulnerability. Express your prayer to God this way and then choose a partner and talk about how you felt. Try to name your feelings.

19. Another expression of self-offering nonverbally in prayer is to raise hands, palms upward, very slowly in front of you, fingers joined together and outstretched. Bring hands together to form a chalice and move it slowly to your chest. Then raise your head heavenward.

20. During Advent invite the congregation to do simple movements to the chorus of a carol, which means "a circle dance." Circles can move by skipping or walking.

21. Observe, explore, and participate in the joy and celebration of the Jewish circle dances, horas of Hanukkah or ritualistic Hasidic movements as danced blessings, Hawaiian and Oriental hand movements, and ancient Spanish, Native American, African, and African-American dances.

22. Take hands, and as you breathe in, raise arms; lower them as you breathe out. Continue this movement in praise of God, Giver of life and breath.

23. Invite the entire congregation to move toward one another (if able), saying, "Thank you for being part of my creation."

24. Movement Toward Breaking the Dividing Wall. Invite a dancer or a mime to do the following: The white-masked man balanced himself on the gray strip of masking tape that lined the floor of our chapel, separating the sanctuary, the pulpit side from the lectern side of the congregation. With great effort he pulled up the tape, pausing between each piece of hard work, raising the "wall" in his hands in celebration, as we prayed the litany of reconciliation. On and on he went, tearing down, destroying the wall, reminding us silently of our divisions. When he had at last, with great anguish and turmoil, torn out even the piece that separated the altar area, he placed them before the cross on the altar and knelt in prayer and penitence while the congregation prayed in silence.

---

1. Marjorie Procter-Smith, *In Her Own Rite: Constructing Feminist Liturgical Tradition* (Nashville: Abingdon, 1990), p. 30.

2. Robert Neale, *In Praise of Play* (New York: Harper & Row, 1969), p. 129.

3. Thomas H. Troeger, *Imagining a Sermon* (Nashville: Abingdon, 1990), p. 30.

4. Dick F. Vieth, *Holy Power Human Pain* (Chicago: Meyer Stone, 1990).

2

Creative Worship

We are people of different temperaments, experiences, needs, and desires, and we learn in different ways. Worship is celebrating God's presence publicly in community and privately in solitude. Worship is the "work" of the people. Because we are different, our work and our worship will vary. "Creative" worship does not mean changing everything every week. "Creative" worship offers choices of different prayers, readings of scripture, drama, music, art, storytelling, choral readings, and so forth to meet the different needs of the worshiping community.

Worship, whether we like it or not, is based on the attitudes of people. Attitudes about worship include the sermon's style and content, the mode of announcements or prayers of concern, children's time (appropriate, inappropriate, or should it happen at all?), the speed of lighting the candles, wearing robes and, if so, what color, to process or not to process, to move the body or sit still, the need for confession and how much, communion every month or why only once a month, and so on.

Rather than "Unless it pleases me, I cannot worship," or "Anything goes," we can substitute critical evaluation, concern, and education in "Why do we do it this way? Can we do it better? What would be more helpful and appropriate? Upon Whom or what are we focusing? Is this aspect of worship relevant and faithful? How do we educate, inspire, heal, and proclaim? What do we need to eliminate or expand?"

Robert H. Mitchell tells the story of a worship service at St. Giles Cathedral to begin the annual world-famous festival of the arts in Edinburgh, Scotland. It was an elegant occasion involving artists of the festival and civic leaders of Edinburgh. The colorful procession of capes and swords, Scottish kilts and scarlet robes and the rich ecclesiastical garments, the organ that shook both the crowd and the building, was the setting in which Dr. Erik Routley was invited to address this very distinguished audience. With great competence the choir sang a very dissonant 12-tone anthem, completely unfamiliar and unfriendly, yet appropriate in this context, focusing on contemporary art. They sang it magnificently. After the service, in a gathering in the fellowship hall, one of the civic leaders commented, "That was a great service, but I didn't care much for the choir music." Routley responded, "You weren't supposed to *like* that anthem."[1]

Are we supposed to *like* each scripture reading, Psalm, sermon, hymn, or anthem? I do not *like* all of Jesus' words. They not only startled and upset the scribes and Pharisees, they startle and disturb me. I do not *like* the cross but it is the foundation of my faith.

How do we reconcile our needs for the new and the old? How do we react to resentment and resistance? How do we maintain "tradition" as well as address the needs and longings of today? What makes music "Christian" or appropriate to worship? How are attitudes formed? What are our experiences with jazz, rock, Mozart's music, didactic or narrative sermons? What factors expand our willingness to experiment and be open to change and growth, paradox and surprise, integral to the Christian message? Some people like silence. Others prefer words. Some like "high," dignified worship, others "low," folksy-friendly worship. What happens when our "idols" and "images" of God will not allow either God or us to change?

When English was introduced into worship in place of Latin, due to the Protestant Reformation, the fact that the people could now understand, participate in, and be educated was not as important as the fear of change, and they protested. In 1976, the Roman Catholic Church did the same, due to the Second Vatican, and the outcry by "those who pay the freight" was great.

To change the "Holy Book," the King James Bible, was a sin, according to the many who forgot or did not know the resistance to this "new" version of 1611. One distinguished seventeenth century British Latin, Greek, and Hebrew scholar wrote about the new "King James" version:

The Authorized Version was sent to me to censure: which bred in me a sadness which will grieve me while I breathe, it is so ill done. Tell his Majesty that I would rather be rent in pieces by wild horses, than that any such translation by my consent should be urged upon the poor churches ... The cockles of the seashores, and the leaves of the forest, and the grains of the poppy may as well be numbered as the gross errors of this Bible.[2]

Two of our famous theologians, John Knox and John Calvin, protested the wearing of costly, jeweled robes. They insisted that they would only wear their working clothes into the pulpit. What were those clothes? Long, black robes with white tabs at the collar.

"O Sacred Head Now Wounded" is a sacred hymn to the worshiper of today. Yesterday it was a secular love song, "My Heart Was Wounded For The Love Of A Fair Maiden." There were no songs in the new Lutheran reformation. It was up to Martin Luther and others to compose them, and they borrowed from the singing around them. Even "Praise God From Whom All Blessings Flow" in the sixteenth century was referred to as a "Geneva jig."

The purpose of images and icons is to point to God. They are "windows" to look through rather than be worshiped. Words and ideas are not holy, not even creeds and doctrines. Nor are they eternal, for all times and every place. It would be sad if all our opinions and beliefs were static. The Christian message is about spiritual growth and transformation, "new life" in Christ. Worship is about God and to God.

On the other hand, I can appreciate the words, " 'Tis mad idolatry that makes the service greater than the god." I have attended worship services in which, because of individual differences and attempts toward becoming inclusive, we worshiped in a variety of ways. From pure silence to body movement, hand clapping, and vocal "Amens" we came to God with our prayers and our praise. Some saw it as entertainment, perhaps even "mad idolatry" that interfered with their worship. C.S. Lewis observed: "As long as you notice, and have to count, the steps, you are not yet dancing but only learning to dance. A good shoe is a shoe you don't notice

... The perfect church service would be one we were almost unaware of; our attention would have been on God."[3]

It is true that the "creative" worship leader (and the uncreative) can get in the way of worship. The unfamiliar can make us aware, move us out of our lethargy, or "make the service greater" than God.

Education is essential. Innovation can be exciting. Congregations who sing only the "good old hymns" are missing the glory of the new ones and robbing the young of their place in the church. Religion and worship are dynamic. Our relationship with God is a living, changing one, therefore our worship will be, as well.

Yet novelty has the danger of fixing our attention on the celebrant rather than on the service of prayer and worship of God. Lewis put it a bit more strongly when he quoted the one who said, "I wish they'd remember that the charge to Peter was Feed my sheep; not Try experiments on my rats, or even, Teach my performing dogs new tricks."

Just as our relationship with God is a paradox — reverent and intimate, transcendent and immanent — so is our worship — formal and informal, new and old. We are simultaneously aware of the intimate nearness of God and the infinite distance in prayer.

Personal prayers are prayers of the heart, the plagues, pains and pleasures of our particular person. No one can pray for us. Yet ready-made, traditional prayers keep us in touch with the community's faith rather than our own personal religion, "my" religion, and help us avoid an irreverent informality.

When it comes to the liturgy, however, the "words" of the service, we are looking at a different question than permanence and uniformity. A vernacular liturgy is a changing liturgy, for living language changes, a new Book of Worship, a new Hymnal, a Revised Version of the Bible are needed and welcome. Revision is for the purpose of intelligibility. Words change in meaning. Rotted words lose their power. Language determines its audience. Words that enlighten one congregation may only confuse another. Archaic expressions are applauded by some and booed by others. Inclusive language is a must for some and a "red flag" for others. How does one please all?

One doesn't. Paul knew the problem and therefore we are blessed by his words: "Now I appeal to you, brothers and sisters, by the name of our Lord Jesus Christ, that all of you be in agreement and that there be no divisions among you, but that you be united in the same mind and the same purpose" (1 Corinthians 10). "We who are strong ought to put up with the failings of the weak, and not to please ourselves. Each of us must please our neighbor for the good purpose of building up the neighbor ... May the God of steadfastness and encouragement grant you to live in harmony with one another, in accordance with Christ Jesus, so that together you may with one voice glorify the God and Father of our Lord Jesus Christ" (Romans 15:1-2, 5-6). We are united in Christ as one body.

So we gather to say as Christ's body his words and his prayer, and though some of us say "debts" and others "trespasses" (both words are out of date), there is unity in our diversity, as we confess our separations, our fears and doubts, our lack of trust and deeds. "This also is Thou: neither is this Thou." Gospel means "good" news and so we will not drown it in lukewarm water or freeze it for posterity, but let it bubble in the life-giving, renewing waters of the Spirit. Made in the image of our Creator, endowed with the gifts of imagination and creativity, we are called to respond with free and joyous, meaningful ways of worship.

---

1. Robert H. Mitchell, *I Don't Like That Music* (Carol Stream, II: Hope Publishing Co., 1993), p. 13-14.

2. F.F. Bruce, *The English Bible* (Oxford: Oxford University Press, 1961), p. 107.

3. C.S. Lewis, *Letters to Malcolm: Chiefly on Prayer* (New York: Harcourt Brace Jovanovich, 1964), p. 4.

3

Calls To Worship

The poet Wallace Stevens wrote that a poet's words are of things that do not exist without the words. Such is true for the service of worship as well. Jesus proclaimed the Kingdom of God through his words and actions, the "good news." The call to worship invites the congregation of faith, gathered in his name, to praise and thank, petition and intercede, confess, hear God's word, and take the bread.

The call to worship calls its people out of the ordinary into the extraordinary celebration of the One who creates, sustains, and guides. On the Sabbath, God completed the work that had been begun. Sabbath begins and ends our work, for worship is the work of the people.

New Year
1. God, hear each resolution, hope, and fear, and bless with gentleness the lion and the lamb, the hawk, the dove, all warring creatures, that this new year our stockpiles may be filled with love. Come, let us worship God who is Love.

Advent
2. The night before Christmas is secrets and smiles,
Noeling and candles on long evergreened aisles
Of churches, cathedrals, welcoming Light,
Their flames celebrating that first Christmas night.
Come, let us worship this night before Christmas.

3. The gift of love begins in the heart of the one who cares,
In the time that it takes to think and plan, as the giver shares.

The gift of love is a simple gift, no matter how great or small,
When the givers offer themselves, the greatest gift of all.
Come, let us worship the One who sent the Son.

4. They slowly came, yet they were turned away
From every door ... "No room to stay!"
If keepers then had known who was their guest,
Would they have found a place for him to rest?
Or did God choose the humble stall
Of hen and cow to show us all
That in our world of pride and greed
Compassion is our greatest need.
Come, let us worship the Christ Child.

5. With eager expectation in great anticipation
We have waited for this night.
With glowing adulation we join with God's creation
To see anew the wondrous sight,
The birthday of this newborn king,
While heaven and earth and angels sing.
Come, let us join in worship!

6. Leader: O come, Light, shining in a dark world,
Fire our minds and imaginations with your heat.
**People: O come, Love at Christmas,
Fill our hearts and homes with your love.**
Leader: O come, Emmanuel, God-with-us,
Be present now and hear our prayers and praises.
All: O come, all ye faithful, and worship the Lord. Amen.

Lent

**7. People: Oh, Lord, in these days we cry to you, "Who are we
and what are we to do?"**
Leader: "I know the plans I have for you, says the Lord, plans for
your welfare and not for harm, to give you a future with hope."
**People: But where are you, Lord, for in these days it seems so
dark and silent?**

Leader: "Then when you call upon me and come and pray to me, I will hear you."

People: But where are you, Lord? You seem to be absent in these days.

Leader: "When you search for me, you will find me; if you seek me with all your heart, I will let you find me, says the Lord...."

All: Come, let us worship and celebrate the presence of the Lord! (Jeremiah 29:11-14a)

8. Minister: Blessed be the name of God for ever and ever, to whom belongs wisdom and might.

People: He gives wisdom to the wise and knowledge to those who have understanding.

Minister: Seek the Lord while he may be found, call upon him while he is near.

People: For great is the Lord, and greatly to be praised.

Minister: Come, let us worship our Lord!

9. "For everything there is a season, and a time for every matter under heaven: ... a time to speak, and a time to keep silence ..." (Ecclesiastes 3:1, 7).

Come, let us worship the LORD our God who speaks in the sheer silence.

10. Leader: Come, let us sing to the Lord;

People: Let us shout to our saving rock!

Leader: Let us enter God's presence with praise.

People: With music and shouts of joy.

All: Let us worship the Lord!

11. God asks us, "Where are you?" God calls us out of the noisy, busy marketplace into the Garden of God's presence to be with our Creator. Come, let us worship Our Lord!

12. Leader: In hope we are were saved.

People: But hope that is seen is not hope.

Leader: We hope for what we do not see.

27

People: We wait for it with patience.
Leader: For the word of the Lord is true.
People: God is faithful to his promise.
Leader: Come, let us worship the LORD.

13. People: How long, O Lord, how long?
Leader: Come, all you who are empty, and be fed.
People: I don't know what I've done or anything in me I can get rid of.
Leader: Come, you who are weak and weary, confused and doubting.
People: I feel I have failed someone or something outside of myself.
Leader: Come, and accept yourself as being accepted by God in spite of being unacceptable. Come, let us worship the God of Jacob who is our refuge.
All: The Lord of hosts is with us.

14. Leader: Come, you who are rich in possessions or love, in food or fellowship, in talents or time, and you who are poor in material things, or education, or job opportunities, in articulation or in the arts, for with God all things are possible.
People: And me?
Leader: And you, and me, let us worship our God!

15. Jesus is coming and going ... going and coming ...
You cannot catch him in your hand
So do not wait until you understand.
Come, let us worship the One who always goes before us.

16. Come, all who are hungry for spiritual food, lonely for unconditional love, diseased, and "near death." Come, let us worship God, our Healer.

17. Faith comes from what is heard, and what is heard comes through the word of Christ. Come, let us hear and worship the Word of God, Christ Jesus, our Lord.

18. Leader: "Since we are justified by faith,
People: We have peace with God through our Lord Jesus Christ,
Leader: And we boast in our hope of sharing the glory of God" (Romans 5:1-2).
All: Come, let us worship the Lord!

19. "If while we were enemies, we were reconciled to God through the death of his Son, much more surely, having been reconciled, will we be saved by his life." Come, let us worship the Lord of our redemption; reconciliation with God.

20. Leader: Behold the mighty acts of God!
People: God is faithful and true.
Leader: Just as Christ was raised from the dead by the glory of the Father,
People: So we too might walk in newness of life.
Leader: If we have died with Christ
People: We believe that we will also live with him.
All: Let us worship the God of our baptism into Christ Jesus.

21. God gives life to the dead and calls into existence the things that do not exist. Therefore we are fully convinced that God is able to do what God promises. Come, let us worship the God of Abraham, the One who raised Jesus our Lord from the dead.

22. Let us worship the Lord. God is our righteous God, abounding in steadfast love to all who call on God.

For God is good and forgiving.

And God is great and does wondrous things.

And God is good and forgiving.

The Lord is slow to anger and abounding in steadfast love and faithfulness and helps and comforts us.

For God is good and forgiving.

"The fear of the Lord is the beginning of wisdom ..." (Psalm 111:10).

Come, let us worship the Lord!

23. "The old things are passed away, behold, they are become new." Come, let us worship God who helps us with transitions and change.

24. Mark wrote that "Jesus spoke all these things to the crowd in parables; he did not say anything to them without using a parable. So was fulfilled what was spoken through the prophet: 'I will open my mouth in parables,
I will utter things hidden since the creation of the world.' "
Come, let us worship God who speaks in sacred stories.

25. "Speak to Him, thou! for He hears, and Spirit with spirit can meet, Closer is He than breathing, and nearer than hands or feet." (Tennyson, "The Higher Persuasion")

26. Leader: Let us thank the Lord for his steadfast love,
People: For his wonderful works to humankind.
Leader: Let us extol him in the congregation of the people,
People: And praise him in the assembly of the elders.
Leader: Come, let us worship the Lord! (from Psalm 107).

27. In the beginning was the Word and the Word was with God and the Word was God. Come, let us worship our God, who created us and speaks to us through the Word.

28. "Then God said, 'Let us make humankind in our image, according to our likeness ...' " (Genesis 1:26). Come, let us worship God, our Creator and our Image.

29. "Where is the dwelling of God?"
This was the question with which the rabbi of Kotzk surprised a number of learned men who happened to be visiting him.
They laughed at him: "What a thing to ask! Is not the whole world full of his glory?"
Then he answered his own question: "God dwells wherever one lets him in."[1]
Come, let us worship and let God in!

30. Bind the strong man,
Stalk the beast,
Transform the powers
That blind and bind
For the end is yet to come.
Birth justice in Christ's name,
Proclaim good news!
Flee to the mountains,
For the sun darkens, the moon dims,
The stars fall from their places,
While the powers in the heavens shake.
The Human One is coming
With great glory
With great power.
Awake! Watch! Wait!
He is near.
He is at the gates.
He is knocking on the door.
Beware! Be aware!
Bind the strong man within, the strong man without!
Come, let us worship the Human One, who is knocking on the door.

31. I came to the healer and he asked, "Why are you here?" and I said, "I feel as if I have within me a withered spirit, a wet dishrag, and I want a strong, firm avocado seed instead."

And he said, "Get up, pick up your mat and walk!"

Come, let us worship the Lord who is Our Healer!

32. As Michelangelo pushed the huge piece of marble down the cobblestoned street to his studio, a child asked, "Why are you pushing that rock?"

"Child," the sculptor replied, "there is an angel in that rock trying to get out."

Come, let us worship God who gives us angels in rocks and eyes to see.

33. A young philosopher, grown despondent in pondering eternity and infinity, could not see how it would matter that he had ever lived. His despair was further compounded when, on an October afternoon on a high hill, he watched a wide valley below ebb and flow with a million swirling leaves. He thought: look at the leaves, nothing but confusion. They swirl and tumble and spin without purpose.

Then the wind quieted and all the millions of leaves settled to lacquer the land. At once he saw that the word "brown" had so many millions of meanings that there were not enough words to describe them. Right then he knew that not one single "red" was precisely like any other, and that the shades of yellow outnumbered the sands, the stones, the stars.

At last he knew that he mattered. He was as much a part of the mystical magic as the beech, butternut, birch, oak, maple, poplar, and each of the trees that had given its leaves to create the grand mosaic of color below.[2]

Come and let us worship the One who makes known that we matter, for we are God's "Somebody."

34. Three men looked at a rock. The first man, impressed with its size, exclaimed, "That is quite a rock!"

The second man, seeing its use, said, "It would make a strong wall."

The third man, seeing its beauty, picked up his tools and chiseled a granite angel from the rock.

Come, let us worship God who transforms "rocks" into "angels."

35. One of the devotees in the temple was well known for his zealousness and effort. Day and night he would sit in meditation, not stopping even to eat or sleep. As time passed he grew thinner and more exhausted. The master of the temple advised him to slow down, to take more care of himself. But the devotee refused to heed his advice.

"Why are you rushing so, what is your hurry?" asked the master.

"I am after enlightenment," replied the devotee. "There is no time to waste."

"And how do you know," asked the master, "that enlightenment is running on before you, so that you have to rush after it? Perhaps it is behind you, and all you need to encounter it is to stand still — but you are running away from it!"[3]

Come, let us worship God in stillness and in trust.

36. The rabbi saw a man in the marketplace so intent upon his business he never looked up. He asked him, "What are you doing?" And the man answered hurriedly, "I have no time to talk to you now." The rabbi, however, refused to be snubbed and repeated his question, "What are you doing?" This time the merchant impatiently cried, "Don't delay me. I have to attend to my business." But the rabbi insisted. "Everything you are so worried about is in the hands of God and all that is in yours is to fear and love God." The man looked up and for the first time knew what the fear and love of God was.

Come, let us worship God in wonder and love of God.

37. The Hasidic rabbi asked his students, "How do we determine the hour of dawn, when night ends and day begins?" One of them replied, "When we can from a distance distinguish a dog from a sheep?" "No," said the rabbi. "When we can distinguish a fig tree from a grapevine?" asked a second. "No," said the rabbi. "Then tell us!" they exclaimed. "It is when you can look into the face of human beings and have enough light in you to recognize them as your sisters and brothers. Until then it is night and darkness is still with us," said the rabbi.

Come and worship God who brings light out of darkness.

38. There is an old rabbinical story that says when the Israelites, wandering in the wilderness, heard the first word of the Law in the Ten Commandments, they swooned, they fainted, they passed out. So the word returned to God and cried out, "O Sovereign of the Universe, You live eternally and your Law lives eternally. But you have sent me to the dead. They do not listen. They do not hear.

33

They are all dead!" Thereupon God had mercy and made God's word more understandable ... God told a story.

Come, let us worship God, the Great Word-Giver.

39. Musical Calls: In a sense musical calls seem to say, "Come out and play," as Jesus said, "We piped to you but you would not dance."

Bells or Celtic rattle: Bells have been a way of calling the worshiper to the place of worship for a long time. I once participated in worship when a woman came down the center aisle with small bells on her wrists and ankles, carrying bells and smiling at the community as she "led" us to the altar and into worship.

Flute: A certain villager used to pray on the Days of Awe in the House of Prayer of the Baal Shem Tov ("Master of the Good Name of God," their leader). His son, who could neither read nor write and was completely ignorant, had a flute on which he would play while watching his flock of sheep. His father never took him to the House of Prayer until the day he became Bar Mitzvah, and then he took him just to make sure he did not eat on the holy fast day. That day the boy sat through Yom Kippur without praying, because he did not know how. "Father," he whispered, "I want to play my flute." His father was aghast and shook his head to refuse the boy. During the Afternoon Prayer the boy asked again, and his father, of course, refused again, this time even holding the boy's pocket so he could not reach his flute. During the Closing Prayer, however, the boy forced the flute from his pocket and played a loud blast. When the Baal Shem Tov heard the sound, he shortened his prayer, saying, "With the sound of his flute this child has lifted up all of our prayers. The flame of his longing kindled a fire within him and because of the strength of his longing, he played the song of his heart truly, for the sole sake of the Name of God."

Shofar: Blown for summoning and ritual purposes. It is a trumpet made of ram's horn to call the people to worship. Today it is sounded in the synagogue at Rosh Hashanah, the beginning of the Jewish New Year (usually late September or early October) and Yom Kippur (Day of Atonement, the holiest Jewish holiday).

34

We celebrate New Year's by blowing paper horns and noise-makers. *(Hand out and blow.)* Whenever you blow your horn on New Year's, remember it is a time to thank God for the old year and for the new one that is to come.

Drum: One way the village "talks." In Africa the drum is designed after the beat of the heart, a communication between the creature and the Creator. Its beat is in time with the Earth and is believed to be a healing instrument. The drum has a processional quality.

40. Jesus saw a woman with a spirit that had crippled her for eighteen years, called her into the midst of them, and said, "Woman, you are set free from your spirit of weakness, your ailment." Come, all who are "bent over," to worship God, who sets us free.

---

1. Martin Buber, *Tales of the Hasidim Later Masters* (New York: Schoken, 1948) and Elaine M. Ward, *Encountering God* (Brea, CA: Educational Ministries, 1990), p. 13.

2. Mel Ellis, *Sermons in Stones* (New York: Holt, Rinehart & Winston, 1975).

3. Christina Feldman and Jack Kornfield, eds., *Stories of the Spirit Stories of the Heart* (San Francisco: Harper, 1991) p. 214.

4

Prayers Of Confession And Assurance

"And the foundations of the thresholds shook at the voice of him who called, and the house was filled with smoke. And I said: 'Woe is me! For I am lost; for I am a man of unclean lips, and I dwell in the midst of a people of unclean lips; for my eyes have seen the King, the Lord of hosts!' " Isaiah *confessed* in the sanctuary in worship.

Worship is humble confession, as we gather together in the fellowship of the church. Some worship houses are filled with pleasant incense and perfumes, sweet-sounding songs amid the cherubic choirs, under brightly shining chandeliers, stained-glass windows, high altars, velvet cushions; other worshipers kneel on bare floors, in steamy fields, hospital corridors, barracks, and barricades. Wherever we worship, we worship with unclean lips. We wonder why leaders of Third World countries, seeing the dire plight of their people, cheat them, as we stuff our own stomachs with coffee grown in their fields, picked by peasants with parched throats and empty stomachs.

"Woe is me!" Isaiah cried. In prayers of confession we are one. Whenever our eyes are opened to the despair, destruction, and death of our brothers and sisters around the world, we see our own woe. In worship we are aware of the needs of others and confess what we have done and what we have not done, for we believe God in mercy forgives.

Confession unites the service of worship with the service of work. It reminds us that the table is set, the banquet ready, but all too often we reserve the chairs for the rich and the strong rather than the poor and those in need, the ones for whom Jesus came, the ones who finally came to God's banquet. There will not be harmony

37

nor health for one until there is justice and peace for all, until we all are seated around the table.

How God acts in Christ is both a sign of God's relationship with us and a means of restoring that relationship. Christ is God's decision: sign and means, offering us the good news of God's unconditional love and forgiveness. God is the Initiator. We are the responder. Christ is the symbol of forgiveness.

1. Leader: A small child found a bird with a beautiful song in the forest and brought it home. But the father did not want to feed a mere bird and so he killed it. And with the bird, he killed the song, and with the song, himself. Forgive us all our thoughtless killings. Awaken us to life. Amen.

Assurance: A Chinese artist painted "The Prodigal Son" with the father waiting at the gate for his approaching son. His friend exclaimed, "That is all wrong. The father should not be standing, waiting, but running to meet his son." "But no Chinese father could do that!" said the artist. "That is just the point! God's amazing love — God loves us like that!" The next painting showed the father running to the son, in shoes that did not match.[1] God is that running, loving Parent.

2. Lord, how can I sing your song in a strange land?
How can I sing your song in a land of babel and bickering and backbiting?
In a land of chaos and crises, loneliness, death, and despair?
How can I sing your song when no one listens or seems to care?
I weep, and suddenly I see the slain Lamb,
And join the heavenly throng
To celebrate your presence in the apathy, and the change,
And in my singing I celebrate me,
And suddenly all I see is changed and charged with song.
I will sing to you who sits on the throne and to the Lamb a new song!
I will praise your name for ever and ever! Amen.

Assurance: God promises "Before I formed you in the womb I knew you ... While you were yet sinners Christ died for you."

3. A dialogue skit for a prayer of confession:

A man knelt at the altar and prayed. "O God," he said, "I am all evil, without and within. My shoulders are bowed with the weight of my sin. God of all mercies, be merciful to me, the chief of sinners!" As he went out he met a friend. "Where have you been?" asked the friend. "I have been at the altar," said the man, "confessing my sins." "Speaking of sins," said the friend, "there is a fault that I have often noticed in you." And he told him of his fault. "Liar!" said the man, and smote him on the mouth.[2] Lord, forgive us for being defensive of the honest, helpful criticism of others. Open our eyes and ears to your correction, so that we may become more obedient and loving and forgiving. In Christ's name. Amen.

Assurance: And God says, "I will love you as you are. I will love you in your defensiveness and in your hearing, for you are my child, whom I have called by name." Amen.

4. "He also told this parable to some who trusted in themselves that they were righteous and regarded others with contempt: 'Two men went up to the temple to pray, one a Pharisee and the other a tax collector. The Pharisee, standing by himself, was praying thus, "God, I thank you that I am not like other people: thieves, rogues, adulterers, or even like this tax collector. I fast twice a week; I give a tenth of all my income." But the tax collector, standing far off, would not even look up to heaven, but was beating his breast and saying, "God, be merciful to me, a sinner!" I tell you, this man went down to his home justified rather than the other; for all who exalt themselves will be humbled, but all who humble themselves will be exalted' " (Luke 18:9-14). In silence and humility, let us pray our prayers of confession.

Assurance: Jesus said, "I know that and I love you."

5. 2 Samuel 12:1-7: David Mammon, chief executive officer of Guaranty Rural Amalgamated Businesses (GRAB), looked over the export-import figures of a small rural country in Central America and realized planting coffee would bring in greater profits than the natives growing food for themselves with only a small portion of export.

Soon the entire countryside became a coffee plantation. Some of the farmers were reemployed by GRAB but their wages were too low to buy enough food for their families, and if they complained, they were fired, and bullets were fired through their homes as well.

One Sunday David Mammon went to church where he sang in the choir and was active in its fellowship. He heard the story of the rich man who took from the poor man all that he had, and David Mammon was incensed. In the coffee-hour afterward, David said heatedly, "He should have had to pay the poor man four times as much as he stole," but there was nó messenger from God to point to David and say, "You are the man."[3]

Assurance: God says, "..I will be merciful toward your iniquities, and I will remember your sins no more" (Hebrews 8:12).

6. There was an old man living in a temple and the demon came to say to him, "Leave this place which belongs to us," and the old man said, "No place belongs to you." Then they began to bother his work and the old man continued with persistence. A little later the devil took his hand and pulled him to the door. When the old man reached the door, he seized the lintel with the other hand, crying out, "Jesus, save me." Immediately the devil fled away. Then the old man began to weep. The Lord said to him, "Why are you weeping?" and the old man said, "Because the devils have dared to seize a man and treat him like this." The Lord said to him, "You had been careless. As soon as you turned to me again, you see I was beside you."[4]

Assurance: "The Lord is gracious and merciful, slow to anger and abounding in steadfast love. The Lord is good to all, and God's compassion is over all that God has made" (Psalm 145:8-9).

7. "Why not?" he asked. I brought up excuses: "Not enough time ... my parents ... my family ... my temperament ... I'm scared ..." There was a sword hanging on the wall. He took it down and gave it to me. "Here, with this sword you can cut through any barriers." I took it and slipped away without saying a word. Back in my room I sat down and looked at the sword. I knew that what he said was true. The next day I returned his sword. How can I live without my excuses?[5]

Assurance: "This is the Lord's doing. It is marvelous in our eyes." And God said, "Let us make man and woman in our image." In God's image, with God's love, we are made. Amen.

8. Too tired to take time to give our thanks,
Too busy to bother with worshiping in the sanctuary,
Too selfish to share our joy with the suffering and the sad,
Too hurt to forgive the one who forgot or caused the pain,
Too frightened to offer the stranger a friendly smile or word,
Too full of self to be faithful to You, O God, who creates, fulfills, and loves.
Dear God, Creator-Parent, we confess our sins of doubt, neglect, and selfishness and we ask You to give us Your forgiveness and Your love.

Assurance: There is a Talmudic story that says when the children of Israel reached the Red Sea, and Moses struck his staff on the shore, the waters of the sea did not part to let them through. The Israelites stood there at the edge of the water and nothing happened until one of the men plunged in. Then the waters rolled back. God was there and God is here now. Plunge in and be assured of God's love.

9. O Eternal One,
Listener
to our roaring in the dark
Singer
with the morning's early stars
Creator
of ribboned-colored rainbows
wrapping gifts of love
Caller
to his tub of Baptism
and his table of Communion
enfold me in Your possibilities
breathe on my imagination

and lead me deeper in and deeper in
until I see all creation
shine with Your presence. Amen.

Assurance: "When I was hungry, you gave me something to eat, when I was thirsty you gave me something to drink, when I needed a home you gave me a place to live. Inasmuch as you have done it to the least, you have done it to me."

Two Prayers Of Confession For Children

10. Sometimes, no matter how I try
To stop, I can't, and have to cry.
When I fall down and skin my knee,
When my best friend is mean to me,
When I can't play and I want to,
And Mother scolds because I do.
When I am tired and quarrel and fight,
And things go wrong from morn 'til night.
Sometimes, no matter how I try
To please, I can't, and wonder "Why?"
It's then I need to know you're there.
Hear, dear Lord, my confession prayer. Amen. (Psalm 106:44)

Assurance: "The fruit of the Spirit is love, joy, peace, patience, kindness, generosity, faithfulness, gentleness, and self-control" (Galatians 5:22-23). Be assured of these gifts in the name of the One who created all good gifts. Amen.

11. Dear Lord, when my friend Fred tells me about
The fish he caught last week,
Small, swaggering soldiers stream outside
My lips with swords to speak,
And when my friend Nancy laughs about
The dress her neighbor wears,
They change to swarms of buzzing bees
That bite and sting in pairs
And some will tease and some will hurt,
And some are simply slips.

O Lord, please put a guard to watch
The doorway of my lips. Amen.[6]

   Assurance: In Jesus' name, you have but to ask. You are forgiven.

12. The poor in spirit are open, willing to receive, to give up old
ways. Only when we are aware that we are missing the mark do we
ask for forgiveness. One cannot be forgiven until that recognition
happens and amends are made. The Rabbi said to his Hasidim: "A
person cannot be redeemed until he recognizes the flaws in his
soul and tries to mend them. A nation cannot be redeemed until it
recognizes the flaws in its soul and tries to mend them. Whoever
permits no recognition of flaws, be it an individual or nation, permits no redemption. We can be redeemed to the extent to which we
recognize ourselves. When Jacob's sons said to Joseph: 'We are
upright men,' he answered, 'You are spies.' But later, when they
confessed the truth with their lips and with their hearts and said to
one another, 'We are guilty concerning our brother,' the first gleam
of their redemption dawned, and overcome with compassion, Joseph turned aside and wept." Forgive us, Lord.

   Assurance: No dress nor suit of clothes will ever be
As lovely as the leaves upon a tree,
As flowers that neither weave nor spin,
And yet are robed more beautiful than royal men.
If God plans for flowers in their finery,
Think how much more God cares for you and me! (Luke 12:27)

13. Leader: Let us pray: Blow the trumpet at the full moon!
It's a feast day!
I led you, my people,
From Egypt, free.
I fed you with honey and bread.
I loved you, my people,
Tenderly,
But you would have nothing to do with me.
People: Oh, if only the blind could see! (Psalm 81)
All: Forgive us, Lord. Amen.

43

Assurance: "I will be with you," God said to Moses, as Jesus said to his friends. Amen.

14. Leader: Dear Creator God, we have polluted your creation and bent your world with the garbage we have accumulated in the product-oriented, materialistic time we have spent here on your planet Earth. Out of your love, help us love and care for Mother Earth, who provides a "lap" for us. Open our eyes so we may be alert and our ears so we may be aware to thank you and to serve you, in Christ's name. Amen.

Assurance: An old man had given his life in service for others and when it was time for the man to die, a friend told him he would not be forgotten. A large stone would be erected as a monument to him. "Monuments are for the dead," said the old man, shaking his head. "What would you have?" they asked him. "A tree," he replied. "What about your epitaph?" The old man smiled as he replied, "If one leaves a living tree, no one will ever have to ask, 'And what did he do?' "

15. Abel, can you hear me?
Do not leave.
Your mother and your father cry,
Even the mountains grieve.
The sky is sick with sorrow,
The wind moans with alarm,
The earth is dry and barren.
Why must we harm
Our sister or our brother, and our God?
Abel, there is evil
And death, now, in the sod (Genesis 4:2b-9).

Most gracious, loving God, we are Cain. Forgive our foolish, evil ways and let us be brothers and sisters to all who need our love. In the name of Christ, who taught us to pray: "Forgive us this day our trespasses, as we forgive those who trespass against us." Amen.

Assurance: "With joy you will draw water from the wells of salvation" (Isaiah 12:3). Be assured you are forgiven. Amen.

16. The small bird, at the onslaught of night,
"Swoops just in time to his remembered tree.
At most he thinks or twitters softly, 'Safe!
Now let the night be dark for all of me.
Let the night be too dark for me to see
Into the future. Let what will be, be.' "[7]
Thy will be done. Amen.

   Assurance: Receive the Holy Spirit and know that your sins
are forgiven in the name of the Spirit of Christ, who lived and died
so that death and all that limits love has been conquered. Amen.

17. God, My mother thought the world was Jell-o.
She had seen it shiver and felt it shake
And refused to eat.
Somewhere I tasted Jell-o for myself,
Discovering it was sweet,
But knowing her aversion
Never ate with her.
Our banquet together is still to come.
Forgive, and unite us in Your love. Amen.

   Assurance: We are members one of another, and as one body
in Christ, we are forgiven, by the mercy of God. Amen.

18. The Spirit of the Lord is upon me
Because the Lord has anointed me.
He has sent me to bring glad tidings to the poor
And to heal the brokenhearted
To proclaim liberty to the captives
And to set the prisoners free
To announce the year of the Lord
And the day of indignation to comfort.
The Spirit of God is upon me, the Spirit of God has anointed me
The Spirit of God has sent me to the poor, to heal.
The Spirit of the Lord is upon me (Luke 4:18).

   This is our prayer of confession and assurance. Amen.

19. The wolf came creeping to the door,
The lamb was at its side.
    Unlikely kin,
    We let them in,
    To eat and rest awhile.
The lion, weary of its reign,
    purred and took off its crown,
    Forgot the law
    Of tooth and claw
    And by the lamb lay down.
We pray, someday we too may live
As if all of us were one,
    And wars shall cease
    And love increase,
And, Lord, thy will be done! Amen.

    Assurance: "Christ is the end of the law so that there may be righteousness, a right relationship between God and creation, for everyone who believes ... For 'Everyone who calls on the name of the Lord shall be saved.' "

20. Will winded his way with his slingshot
And now the bird is still.
While over the meadow its mate cries,
    "Whip poor Will!"
        Whip poor Will!"
            Whip poor Will!" (Psalm 10:8b)

    Assurance: The psalmist sang, "The Lord is my shepherd," and Jesus said God is our loving Parent. We love because God first loves us.

21. My shoes no longer fit, for my feet are growing.
They pinch my toes and cause me to walk in pain
Until I purchase new ones.
How long before I free my growing Soul
From these too narrow thoughts
That blister until they bleed?
Forgive and grant me courage, in Christ's name. Amen.

Assurance: Jesus says, "Come unto me all you who are weary and lonely, and I will give you rest and the assurance of my love." Amen.

22. Trust is a tender thing, a risk,
The greatest risk that life can bring,
The pain, the fear that love will die,
And yet I know not trust, nor love,
Unless I try. Dear Lord, forgive my lack of trust in Your love. Amen.

Assurance: You are forgiven in the name of God who gives us bread and in Christ Jesus who is the bread and the Holy Spirit who empowers us to be fed and to feed. Amen.

23. Colin Jooste, a South African, tells the story of being black and growing up in South Africa, reading Martin Luther King's banned book, *Strength to Love*, in hidden, remote hideouts, from which his dream for freedom was born. When he was eight years old a white girl threw a ball at him and he caught it. When her white father saw what had happened, he became extremely abusive. Out of fear and frustration Colin's black father smashed his fist into his son's face, and though neither child, white nor black, understood, the future of Colin's theological-existential reality was born. Lord, forgive us, black and white. Amen.

Assurance: Jesus said that the good shepherd calls his sheep by name. Know now that God loves us, forgives us, and calls us by name. Oh, the depth of the riches of the wisdom and knowledge of God. Amen.

24. Dear God, forgive our discontent, the time we waste, the begs and bribes we make to you, the wealth we hoard and withhold from others, even the thoughts that because we have material possessions we are more favored and loved by you. We look for our status, our security, our happiness in wealth. Yet we know the call of Jesus is to a deeper relationship, the call to trust you rather than success or security, for you are on the side of the sufferers. With the rich man who came to Jesus, asking, "What must I do?" we too worry, recognizing our emptiness, disappointment, and disillusionment. Fill us and forgive us, in Christ's name. Amen. *(Silence.)*

Assurance: The disciples asked, "Then who can be saved?" Jesus said, "For mortals it is impossible, but not for God; for God all things are possible."

25. Dear Lord, forgive us for being heavy with the heaviness of the world in our thinking and in our doing. Lift our spirits, fill us with joy and the sense of your love and presence, your plan and promise. In Christ Jesus we believe and pray these words.

Assurance: Jesus said, "I am the resurrection and the life. Those who believe in me, even though they die, will live, and everyone who lives and believes in me will never die." Wherever Jesus is, there is life. Believe this, for these words are true.

26. Dear Lord, you were taken away from us and we feel your absence. We confess that in your absence we feel helpless, hopeless, and powerless. We forget your words to the disciples that you would send the Spirit. Forgive our lack of boldness in the Spirit to be your witnesses to the ends of time. Amen.

Assurance: "This Jesus, who has been taken up from you into heaven, will come in the same way as you saw him go into heaven." Know that Christ Jesus is always going before you, binding up brokenness so that you are loved and you are forgiven. Amen.

27. *(1-3 read from congregation)*
(1) He said to me, "You are beautiful." I ran from him. You see, I am not beautiful. I lack love.
(2) He said to me, "You are strong and brave." I ran from him. You see, I am weak and lack courage.
(3) He said to me, "You are wise and do things well." I ran from him because I fail and he does not know.
All: Forgive me for running, for doubting, being weak and lacking courage and wisdom. Amen.

Assurance: *(All)* **We ran and in our running we met God and one another, and when we stopped long enough to look at each other and to listen to each other and to God, we saw the**

beauty and the strength and the courage in each of us. Then we experienced his words, "I love you as you are." Thanks be to God! Amen.

28. Lonely shepherd on the hill,
Unlearned, untrained, untaught, except by God,
And then an eager student, Amos of Tekoa,
Left his legacy of words.
But who heeds or needs a simple shepherd, come to town to sell his sheep?
Who listens to the rants and ravings of a wild one on the crowded, downtown city streets?
With all the words the Western world has banked, why save these slender images of an unknown peasant of the past,
Especially when they cut and tear and pierce the human heart with painful truth?
Can ancient, Eastern words and thought reflect our own?
Our pews are soft, the kneeling benches carpeted, the music stirring to the spirit.
This is no place for doom-evoking prophets!
The stench of dung among the coiffured, sweet-perfumed and lotion-laden gentlemen and women is offensive to our taste
And inappropriate in our organed, chandeliered, and stain-glassed sanctuary.
We come to church for comfort, not despair, to feed and not be fed upon.
A dirty shepherd's cries of doom cast doubts and gloom upon our anxious age.
Oh, Amos, leave, or touch your truth with pity so we may hear and still pretend to care.
We are too frail to face the judgments of the past.
If we should listen to your words, how could we live?
Shepherd of Tekoa, preach, but not too long or loud, for we must feed our children and care for our friends from what small substance we can call our own.
Yes, Amos, speak, for speak you must, as we must hear, but do not judge too harshly when we cry and close our ears against the truth.

49

We care, Oh, Amos, yes, we care, and yet the burden of our guilt
we cannot bear.
Amos, speak, and God, forgive! (Amos 5:21-24)

Assurance: God assures us through God's sacred story of his
promise, "I will be with you." You are forgiven.

29. Sometimes we, who think we order life,
Recall our place,
When asses see angels on their path,
While we are too blind to recognize God's face
In those we meet who need our love,
Too blind to see the helpless who need our care,
The lonely our company.
Dear God, help me be as aware as Balaam's ass,
And do not let me pass
Until I see Thee everywhere. (Numbers 22:15-35)

Assurance: Hear the final words of the psalmist who first prayed
our prayer of confession: "The Lord did not hide his face from me,
but heard when I cried to him, for he did not despise or abhor the
affliction of the afflicted." In Christ's name, we are forgiven. Amen.

30. Emmanuel, we confess that we have built walls of prejudice
because we fear too many strangers coming, too many aliens making too many things new, too much "news" making life uncom-
fortable. We have built walls of separation even among those who
love us because we are afraid of rejection. We have built walls of
separation even against you because we are afraid of your love.
What would it mean if we accepted your love, accepted ourselves,
accepted the unknown and the new? We are afraid. Let us keep our
walls. Let us live alone, afraid, in fear behind them, but come among
us and take them slowly down piece by piece so that you can be
with us, and hug us, and hold us by our hand, when we still hold on
to fear. We ask this in your name, Emmanuel, knowing the meaning of that name: God with us.

Assurance: What we have done cannot be undone, but "God
cares about you." Amen.

31. Once, just before New Year's, the Baal Shem Tov came to a certain town and asked the people who read the prayers there in the Days of Awe. They replied that this was done by the rav of the town. "And what is his manner of praying?" asked the Baal Shem Tov. "On the Day of Atonement he recites all the confessions of sin in the most cheerful tones," they said. The Baal Shem Tov sent for the rav and asked him the cause of this strange procedure. The rav answered: "The least among the servants of the king, he, whose task it is to sweep the forecourt free of dirt, sings a merry song as he works, for he does what he is doing to gladden the king." And the Baal Shem said, "May my lot be with yours."[8]

Assurance: Other seed fell in good soil and grew up and yielded thirty, sixty, and a hundredfold. Jesus listens to our confession and says, "I know that and I love you."

32. The boy was playing hide-and-seek with another boy. He hid himself and stayed in his hiding place for a long time, knowing his friend was looking for him. Finally, after a long time, he left his place and saw that his friend was gone. His hiding had no meaning, for no one looked for him at all. He ran into the study of his grandfather, crying and complaining about his friend. His grandfather broke into tears and said, "God, too, says: 'I hide, but there is no one to look for me.' "

Dear God, forgive us for not looking for You, the source of all things, the One for whom all things stand. Help us not to hide from You and make us aware and worthy of Your presence. Amen.

Assurance: Jesus says, "God cares for you."

33. We gather this day, O God, to remember and celebrate that you are a God of liberation and justice and to ask your forgiveness. As Creator, we know You to be one who rejoices with us in the beauty and bounty of all creation; as Redeemer, we know you to be the one who weeps with us over the violence of human suffering; and as Sustainer, we understand you to be one who is angered with us at human indifference. Forgive us our sins of evil and of complacency.

Assurance: God says, "I have loved you with an everlasting love" (Jeremiah 31:3).

34. Dear God, there is sadness in seeing small birds behind bars, remembering their brothers who are free to see the stars. Forgive our caging children or clipping their wings or covering their eyes from seeing with imagination and with faith. Amen.

Assurance: The God of hope forgives you and fills you with all joy and peace in believing, so that you may abound in hope by the power of the Holy Spirit.

35. Dear Lord, Forgive our illusions, addictions, and compulsions so that we will not renounce them but simply drop our desire for them.

Help us concentrate on the Now so we can release our hopes for Tomorrow. Transform our attachments, desires, and cravings into energy for Your Kingdom today. In Christ's name. Amen.

Assurance: God cares for the flowers of the field and the birds of the air. How much more God cares for you.

36. Forgive our wandering thoughts, our wayward feet, our weary words, the way we predict and plan and proclaim rather than patiently awaiting Your unpredictable presence. We are people who want to choose and control rather than love and be loved by Your grace and mercy, in Christ our Lord.

Assurance: We sit now in silence, allowing your presence and your love to surround us, as we breathe in your love and peace, and breathe out our worry and hurry. We listen to our breathing as we remember and reflect upon the words, "God breathed into him the breath of life." *(Silence.)* "You are forgiven and given new breath. In Christ's name you are a new creature. Amen."

Advent

37. From home and hearth and hostel turned away,
They found a simple stable and some hay,
A symbol of the way we still refuse

52

The needy from our hearts, and homes, and pews.
Lord, we ask your forgiveness this Advent. Amen.

Assurance: God says, "I call you 'beloved.' You are the objects of my mercy."

38. Dear Creator-Redeemer, forgive us this Advent for not taking time to make room for you in our hearts. Our raucous inns are filled with revelry and mirth that shut you out. Yet our revelry leaves us empty; our progress does not satisfy, our prosperous land is not the promised land of our longing. Forgive us for not becoming humble and filled with hope, for not following the star to your humble manger to share with and love those who are in need, as you did and do so today. In Christ's name we pray. Amen.

Assurance: Jesus said, "Heaven and earth will pass away, but my words will not pass away. But about that day or hour no one knows ... only the Father" (Mark 13:31-32). "And remember, I am with you always, to the end of the age" (Matthew 28:20b).

Lent

39. Dear Lord, we are filled with every kind of wickedness, evil, covetousness, malice, envy, murder, strife, deceit, craftiness, as gossips, slanderers, God-haters, insolent, haughty, boastful inventors of evil, rebellious toward parents, foolish, faithless, heartless, ruthless, and we deserve to die (Romans 1:29-31). Out of the depths we cry: forgive us, O merciful Lord, as we speak our personal confession to you in silence. Amen.

Assurance: God loves and forgives you, as Paul wrote: "... I am convinced that neither death, nor life, nor angels, nor rulers, nor things present, nor things to come, nor powers, nor height, nor depth, nor anything else in all creation, will be able to separate us from the love of God in Christ Jesus our Lord" (Romans 8:38-39).

40. Confession is the way we stumble into God's presence. In silence, let us speak those words we need to say now. *(Silence.)*

Assurance: If the lily and the sea can be reflections of divinity, How much more can human tenderness, a gentle touch, a warm caress! If the sun and sky and singing bird can bring to us God's loving word, How much more Christ, forgiving us through eternity!

41. Only when we are aware that we are missing the mark do we ask for forgiveness. Forgive us, Lord.

Assurance: God said to Joseph's brothers, "You meant it for evil, but I meant it for good."

42. Prayer changes people and people change things. The minister reported a call after his religious radio service from a woman who complained about her unhappiness. Her husband had changed his job. They had moved to a small apartment. Her neighbors were unfriendly. The minister had not yet called. What should she do? He suggested that she confess her sins. "What sins?" she asked. "My friend, self-pity has been coming through this telephone wire for five minutes. I am sitting in three inches of it." "But I can't get to church. I have high blood pressure." "There is radio ..." he replied, adding under his breath, "Dear God, forgive me for putting myself first." The woman promised to use the prayer of absolution and to phone the following week. When she did, she said that her neighbors were friendly, there was lots to do, her blood pressure was down twenty points, and asked, "Aren't you surprised?" "Not at all," he said. "I would have been surprised if you had been your same old unhappy self."[9]

Assurance: Jesus says, "Go and do likewise."

43. Leader: As disciples of the Word,
We confess that too often we are hesitant to speak Your word,
To uproot and tear down evil structure,
To destroy and overthrow injustice,
To build and to plant peace and equality,
To feed Your lambs and take care of Your sheep.
People: Have mercy upon us, O God.
Assurance: "I am with you. I will rescue you," says the Lord.

44. The Lord asks, "Who will be my voice, my words?"

Forgive us, Lord, for babbling, for filling the silence of Your presence with the noise of our many words. In that silence let Your Word come among us now. Amen.

The Lord asks, "Who will be my hands?"

Forgive us, Lord, for empty hands. Reach out Your hand and touch our mouths and our feet so that we may speak and act for You. Put your words in our mouths to tear down and to build up. In the name of the One who reconciles. Amen.

Assurance: Jesus said that when we love God and our neighbor as ourself we are forgiven and we are not far from the kingdom of God.

45. Lord, we struggle in prayer as if we were strangers of the Spirit. Our words crawl and lie in heaps at your feet. Our spirit slumbers. Awaken us to the awe of your presence and accept our silence praise and thanksgiving.

Assurance: Jesus said, "I have come so that the loser wins, the least becomes greatest, the liberated sing and dance, and the poor are filled. Rest, therefore, in the assurance of my love."

46. A man gives a *diram* to each of four persons. The Persian said he would spend his on an *angur*, while the Arab said he would spend his on an *inab*. A Turk said he would spend his on an *uzum,* and a Greek said he would spend his *diram* on an *istabil*. These people began to fight with one another, not knowing that each had in common the desire to purchase a grape.[10]

Lord, forgive our battling to have our own way. Give us the patience to learn to understand one another and to have compassion.

Assurance: Believe the Good News: In the name of Jesus Christ, you are forgiven. Glory to God! Amen!

47. There was once a Capuchin monk, Saint Ignatius of Sardinia, who would beg for money for the poor from the people of the town. He refused, however, to beg from one merchant who had gained his fortune by defrauding the poor. The merchant was furious, for he feared what the people would think, and so he complained to the monk's superior. Ignatius was ordered to make sure that he begged from the merchant the following day. "I will go as you ask, Father, I will go to the merchant, but I will not ask him for alms." The following day the merchant received Ignatius graciously, giving him a large donation and asking him to come to his home again. Ignatius put the sack on his shoulder and left the rich man's house, and as he did, drops of blood dripped from the sack. They ran down the merchant's doorstep and onto the street all the way to the monastery. When he reached the monastery, he laid the sack at the Father's feet. "What is this?" asked the Father. "This," said Ignatius, "is the blood of the poor."[11]

Forgive us, Lord, for taking the "blood of the poor" by the way we use the resources of our planet, by ignoring the orphan and the widow, the poor and the lonely. Forgive us in the name of the One who loved all.

Assurance: Rejoice in the Lord always. Have no anxiety about anything, "but in everything by prayer and supplication with thanksgiving let your requests be made known to God" (Philippians 4:4-9).

48. We have been baptized and put on Christ Jesus, and yet we need continuously to repent and receive forgiveness, for we are a fearful people. We do not know how to love and yet each of us wants unconditional love, acceptance, and assurance. We feel as if we are stoned into a tomb from which there is no escape except by love.

Assurance: Love moves the stone before the entrance of our tomb and enters the emptiness we have prepared. There is therefore now no condemnation for those who are in Christ Jesus. For the law of the Spirit of life in Christ Jesus has set us free from the law of sin and of death. Thanks be to God! Amen.

49. I sometimes have a pain in my left shoulder blade. It used to make me angry. "Go away!" I would shout. Then I would meditate it "out." One day, however, when the sudden ache burst on me uninvited, I said without thinking, "What do you want, God?" I now think of the pain as the way I see God tapping me on the shoulder to get my attention. I do not blame God for the pain. I only thank God for the awareness. I wonder if God used Paul's "thorn of the flesh" to get his attention. I think it worked.

Lord, forgive our "bellyaches and backaches," our complaints, transforming them into revelations. Amen.

Assurance: God says, "You have my promise. I will be with you always."

50. A seabird flew into the palace courtyard of the king, and the king admired the beauty of the seabird and wanted to keep it. He killed a buffalo and gave the meat to the seabird. He had his musicians play fine music and his servants preen the bird and speak admiring words to the bird of its beauty. The bird was caged in a magnificently adorned room, and the seabird died. Forgive us for caging our children, our creatures, and our compassion. In Christ's name, we pray. Amen.

Assurance: Jesus says, "I know that and I love you."

---

1. Elaine M. Ward, *Encountering God* (Brea, CA: Educational Ministries, 1990), p. 49.

2. Laura Richards, *The Golden Windows* (Darby, PA: Darby Books).

3. Robert McAfee Brown, *Unexpected News: Reading the Bible with Third World Eyes* (Philadelphia: Westminster Press, 1984).

4. Benedicta Ward, *The Sayings of the Desert Fathers* (London: Mowbrays, 1975), p. 61.

5. Theophane the Monk, *Tales of a Magic Monastery* (New York: Crossroad, 1980).

6. Elaine M. Ward, *Love in a Lunchbox: Poems and Parables for Children at Worship* (Nashville: Abingdon, 1996), p. 140.

7. Robert Frost, "Acceptance," *Complete Poems of Robert Frost* (New York: Henry Holt & Co., 1949).

8. Martin Buber, *Tales of the Hasidim* (New York: Schocken, 1940).

9. J. Moulton Thomas, *Prayer Power* (Waco, TX: Word Books, 1976).

10. Jim Fowler, Sam Keen, *Life Maps* (Waco, TX: Word Books, 1970).

11. Dorothy Day, *The Catholic Worker,* September, 1979.

5

Scripture Readings For Worship

The Bible is the textbook, the source of guidance and strength, direction and spiritual growth, the heart of Christian worship.

Sometimes
the preacher
of words,
restless and
divinely discontent,
Jacob-like,
struggles with
these angelic creatures
until they name ...
Sometimes
the preacher stands aside
waiting,
listening
for what these divine words
have to say ...
And sometimes
patiently,
gently,
the preacher leads them
as a flock
beside still water.

The word of God is dynamic, living and active, discerning the thoughts and intentions of the heart (Hebrews 4:12). It points us to something that happens in the text and asks us to proclaim from the text the word-event. The aim of the text is to proclaim, encounter, and hand on the proclamation of what has taken place so that it may become the proclamation that takes place here and now.

I have used poetry to interpret many of the texts. Poetry is made of verbal symbols, which are intuitive ideas that have not yet been formulated in any other or better way. Poets write to express what they are thinking, feeling, intuiting, and interpreting in order to give meaning, value and purpose to what is visible and invisible, what is beyond this limiting earth. They help us feel and think.

1. Psalm 139:9-10: "If I rise on the wings of the dawn, if I settle on the far side of the sea, even there your hand will guide me, your right hand will hold me fast." The young sailor, lying in his snow hut at the North Pole, read in his Bible, "If I take the wings of the morning, and fly to the uttermost parts of the sea, even there Thou art with me, and Thy right hand shall uphold me," and under the influence of that faith, sleep came upon him, and dreams, which are the manifestations of God to the spirit. Faraway his grandmother and the woman he loved read the letter that had arrived from the cold regions of the north and they laughed and wept over it, while he, under ice and snow and the shadow of the angel's wings, wept and smiled with them in spirit, for he saw and heard it all in his dream. Then the vision fled and it was dark in the snow hut, but the Bible still rested under his head, and faith and hope dwelt in his heart, for God was with him, even in the uttermost parts of the sea.[1]

2. Invite a person from the congregation to read the scripture for the day from where he or she is rather than at the lectern.

3. The Shema, Deuteronomy 6:4-9: Hear, O *(name of congregation)*, the Lord our God is one *(hands in prayer position)*.
And you shall love the Lord with all your heart *(cover heart)*.
And all your mind *(point to head)*.
And all your strength *(hand clenched)*.

And you shall teach these commandments *(extend Bibles)* to your children when you lie down *(close eyes)* and when you rise up *(stand on tiptoes)* and when you walk in the way *(walk in place)*.

And you shall wear them as frontlets between your eyes *(point to brow)*, these stories *(extend Bibles)* of God's saving acts in history.

And you shall put them on your doorpost and your altars *(place Bible on altar)* and your bulletin board in order to see them when you go out and when you come in.

4. A Delicate Aroma: John 12:1-8
The perfume of sacrifice permeates the room,
But sacrifice is such a heavy odor.
This odor contains the lightness of love and laughter,
Martha's hilarity in the kitchen as she serves,
Lazarus' awareness of resurrection,
The joyous fulfillment of Jesus' message,
The everydayness of deception, betrayal,
Mixed with the possibility of forgiveness.
Perhaps "to carry one's cross,"
The symbol of God's amazing greening love
Is to follow our calling,
For what is perfume for,
This costly nard with which she bathes his feet
And wipes them with her hair,
But love?
    A simple story,
    a call
    to be the aroma of God,
    a delicate aroma,
    an elusive dream,
    all one's own.

5. "His Name Is John" Luke 1:5-23, 57-79:
Out of the darkness
    a song was sung

Out of the silence
    a son was born
And his name shall be called John.
In the silent sanctuary the angel spoke to the priest Zechariah,
Singing the "good news" of God.
But Zechariah,
    the priest of God,
    the leader of God's people
    the keeper of God's holiness
                         feared
                               And was silenced.

Speechless, he listened.
Wrapped in silence
The Spirit spoke
    "His name is John."
Out of the silence
    the heavens and earth were born
Out of God's silence came the Word
    to a waiting world.
Zechariah's speechlessness was a waiting.
Silence precedes the act of naming.
Zechariah floated in silence before he spoke
"His name is John."
When the prophet was named
The priest's tongue was loosed.
Filled with the Holy Spirit, he sang.
In praise the priest proclaimed,
"Blessed be the Lord God of Israel."
Before the word
    the silence
Out of the silence
    the birth
What then is our silence birthing?
Yours and mine?
I cannot speak for you
    but silence births my naming.

And in that naming
     there is life lived in the name of God,
Whose silence births creation
And guides our feet upon the path of peace.

6. Once upon a time there was a man named John ...
John the Baptist?
John the Beloved?
John the Disciple who would not die?
John the writer of 1 John or the Gospel of John or the Book of
Revelation of John? Friend of Paul, or Clement?
Which John? Who John? Why John?
There it is ... Why, John?
Who shares the scholar's story?
Did the author of John write out of ignorance of the other Gospels
... to supplant the other Gospels ... to tell the story, his story, of who
this man, this Lamb of God, really was?
Why does the reader read?
The hearer hear?
The loved one love?
I seek Jesus of Nazareth ...
He is not here. He has risen!
Now he is Light in darkness,
Now he is Bread and Wine,
Shepherd and Gate,
Teacher, Redeemer, Friend of Lazarus,
The Way, the Truth, the Life,
The true Vine,
The pray-er betrayed, the Crucified.
Who are you to me?
"Woman, why are you crying? Who is it you are looking for?"
"Feed my lambs. Behold, the Lamb of God!"
John, the writer, I have read.
John, who testifies, I have heard.
I do not understand your words
But I will follow the Lamb of God
Who said ..."Feed my sheep!"

7. Mark 4:34: "... He did not speak to them except in parables...."

In the beginning Truth walked about the streets as naked as the day he was born. People were surprised and shocked and ran away and shut their doors and would not let Truth into their homes. Truth was unhappy and wandered through the streets sadly. In his great loneliness he met Parable. Parable was dressed handsomely in fine new clothes and was a sight to see. When Parable saw Truth, Parable asked, "What is the matter with you? Why do you walk about the streets naked and dejected?" Truth shook his head sadly and replied, "Everything is wrong for me. I have become old and so the people ignore and avoid me." "What you are saying does not make any sense," Parable replied. "People are not ignoring you because you are old. Look at me. I am as old as you are. Nevertheless, the older I become, the more attractive people find me. But I will tell you a secret about people. They do not like things plain and bare but dressed up prettily. I have an idea. I will lend you some of my clothes and you will soon see how people will welcome you." Truth followed Parable's advice and put on some of his bright clothes, and lo and behold, people no longer shunned Truth but welcomed Truth heartily, and since that time Truth and Parable have been inseparable, loved and esteemed by all.

8. Proverbs 1:7: The fear of the Lord is upon us.
The time for remembering has come.
The mountains shout God's majesty.
Earth shows forth God's honor.
The merciful flowers bloom
And the seas and heavens endure forever.
The faithful grain begins to sing,
And all God's wonderful works join in the chorus,
"Holy is God's name!"
In fear we remember God's promise and power.
This is the beginning of wisdom.
This is understanding.

9. Psalm 23: I find inside myself an angry child
irritated by "wise" advice and strangling demands

of sleeping, parroting, parochial priests
while longing for the wiser words of gentle folk
unbinding my feet to dance,
my heart to sing, my hand to write.
I hold them all at arm's length
and watch them war within,
observing in the tension the creativity.
The Shadow and the Self in step.
Sometimes they waltz in harmony
Sometimes they crumble wearily,
Exhausting the body, they seek release.
I call God the Great Unknown
until in pain and agony I cry
"Our Parent," and "My Shepherd!"

10. How high must I go to find you, O Lord?
How low must I descend?
For neither the passage of time nor space can contain you,
Beyond all thought, all understanding,
Yet nearer than the breath we breathe,
The longings we feel.
The word is near, upon our lips
And in our hearts. (Romans 10:6-8)

11. Luke 6:20-35:

Blessed are you unheard, for you are heard by God.

Blessed are you that study now, for you shall learn.

Blessed are you when you tell God's story and your audience wiggles and squirms. Rejoice in that day, and leap for joy, for behold, your reward is great in heaven; for so their fathers did to their storytellers.

But woe to you that will not use your imagination, for you will fail.

Woe to you that are silent, for you shall report to God.

Woe to you that spend your time before the television screen, for you shall see nothing.

But I say to you, "Tell your story, speak God's word, share God's love. To him who does not listen, learn to meet his needs; and from him who steals your story, give him another as well. And as you wish that preachers would tell you, tell to them."

If you tell stories to those who are interested, what credit is that to you? For all storytellers can tell stories to those who love them. And if you tell someone else's story as if it were your own, what credit is that to you? Even unbelievers read the Bible. But read God's story, believe and let God's story become your own, live and tell God's story to listeners and non-listeners alike, and your reward will be great, and you will be sons and daughters of the Most High; for God is kind to the storyteller, because God loves a good story.

12. Luke 7:41-43: A certain storyteller had two stories, one which he had carefully chosen and prepared and one that he had not. When it was time to tell his story, he told them both. Now which of the two will be enjoyed most?"

"The one, I suppose, that had been prepared."

And he said to him, "You have answered rightly."

13. Luke 10:25: And behold, a preacher stood up to put him to the test, saying, "What shall I do to become a storyteller?"

He said to him, "What is written in the books? How do you read?"

And he answered, "You shall choose a story you enjoy, a story that will heal your hearers; plan, prepare, and share your story carefully."

And he said to him, "You have answered right; do this, and you will be a storyteller." But he, desiring to perfect his art, said, "But who is a storyteller?"

The teacher replied, "A child was coming to church school to learn about God's love and sat among his classmates to listen to the story eagerly. Now by chance the woman who taught his class had a story she had found in the Bible and she read it to him. But he did not understand the ancient, abstract words. So likewise, the man who taught the class had a story from the Bible and though he told the story, he did not really believe it himself. He was neither enthusiastic nor comfortable nor did he identify with the story.

But a teenager helping in the class came to where the child was; and when she saw the child's need to hear God's story, she had compassion, and went to him and told him a story of God's great love and what it had meant to her and could mean to him, and she told the child, "Take care of the story, think about it and let it become your story and next Sunday I will tell you more stories from the Bible that you may feel and think about." Now which of these three, do you think, proved storyteller to the child who needed to hear God's story? And the preacher said, "The one who told the story from the Bible in which the child encountered God at his level, because it was his story."

"Go and do likewise."

14. Luke 12:16-21: And he told them a parable, saying, "The collection of stories of the storyteller grew; and he thought to himself, 'What shall I do, for I have nowhere to store my stories?' And he said, 'I will do this: I will pull down my bookshelves, and build larger ones; and there I will store my stories. And I will say to my soul, Soul, you have ample stories laid up for many years; take your ease, eat, drink, be merry.'

But God said to him, 'Fool! This night your soul is required of you, and the stories you have collected, whose will they be? So is he who lays up stories for himself, and does not share God's story with others.' "

15. Luke 13:5: And he told this parable: A man had a story, and he came telling his story, but no one would listen. And he said to the storyteller, "Lo, these three years I have come telling this story and no one listens. Forget it; why should I use up my memory?" And the storyteller answered him, "Tell it again this year also with enthusiasm and put in pauses. And if it is listened to next year, well and good; but if not, you can forget it."

16. "God who sits in the heavens laughs" (Psalm 2:4a).
He, who sits in the heavens, hears

Our praises and our prayers.
He, who sits in the heavens, shares
Our sorrows and our cares.
He, who sits in the heavens, sees
And laughs with us in mirth.
He, who sits in the heavens, loves
So much he came to earth.

17. John 21:15-17: Do you love me, you of many words,
broken vows and promises,
on whose word I will build my church?
The tongue persuades easily,
the word of truth is harder and less in evidence
in all of life.
Do you love me, bold one,
wielder of the sword,
defender of my honor and my life?
The sword persuades easily,
the deed of truth is harder and less in evidence
in all of life.
Do you love me, more than these?
Love persuades easily,
The laying down of life is harder and less in evidence
in all the world.
Do you love me
with word or sword or life?
Feed my sheep!

18. Psalm 42:1-3: The lonely deer has lost his way
And longs for flowing streams,
Where he can drink and rest awhile
Upon a bed of greens.
Sometimes I, too, feel lonely-lost,
When everything goes wrong,
And I am thirsty for your love.
O Lord, how long? How long?

19. Psalm 8:1: There's splendor in the sound of it
And music when it's said.
It shines and sparkles on the tongue
As starlight overhead.
There's grandeur in the sound of it
And dignity and might,
And I am always dazzled by
The glory of its light.
There's power in the sound of it,
And strength, as we proclaim,
"O Lord, our Lord, of all the earth,
Majestic is thy name!"

20. "Let the words of my mouth and the meditation of my heart be
acceptable in thy sight, O Lord, my rock and my redeemer" (Psalm
19:14).
Let the words of my mouth as country roads
Revive and rest
The weary, as they trudge along *the way.*
Those words are best
That warm the cold and loneliness
Of strangers with their spark
Of friendliness.
Those words that bless the grieving
And give redress, relieving
Wrong and pain.
Those words that like the rain
Feed and refresh.
Let those words be my words,
True and right,
And may the meditations (more words)
Of my heart, O Lord,
Be worthy in your sight.

21. "The people who walked in darkness have seen a great light"
(Isaiah 9:1-16): The car sliced the darkness of the night,
Aiming toward the one small glimmering light

That shone beside the lonely road,
An invitation that meant warmth and food and sleep,
And especially fellow company,
The sound of voices talking, laughing,
The smell of burning firewood,
The sight and taste of smiles and cocoa
Simmering on the stove and in the cup —
All in that one small window light.
Once long ago
Another light shone
To lead us home
Into our Father's loving company.

22. 1 Corinthians 13: If I worship with interruptions and have not love, I gain nothing.

> If I hear the "message for the day," but do not take my child to worship, what does it profit me?
>
> If I am able to concentrate but exclude children, I am nothing.
>
> Love is patient, it allows curiosity: "What are they doing now?"
>
> Love is kind: "Here is paper for you to draw what you hear."
>
> Love is not rude nor selfish: "Please whisper, others are listening."
>
> Love encourages children to stand when others stand, sing when others sing, be silent when others are silent.
>
> Love does not ignore nor scold nor constantly say "shhhhh!"
>
> Love lets children share my hymnal, put their own offering in the plate, shake the pastor's hand.
>
> Love always protects, always trusts, always hopes, always perseveres.
>
> When I was a child, I whispered as a child. I wiggled as a child, I asked questions as a child.
>
> When I became an adult, I helped children worship by involving them in the worship service.
>
> And still these three remain: faith, hope, and love, but the greatest of these is love.[2]

23. Psalm 147:8b: So straight
And still
The grasses grow,
So green upon the hill,
I whispered to the Gardener,
"Thanks,"
And then I, too, was still.

24. Luke 5:1-11: "Put out into the deep water and let down your nets for a catch ... From now on you will be catching people."
 Because of a crowd, there was a catch.
 Because of a catch, there was a call.
 Because of a call, there was a commitment.
 And the crowd and the catch and the call and the commitment were all
 Because there was ... a Christ.
They crowded upon him to hear the word of God.
As greedy spectators impatient for a seat,
As starving children plead for meat,
They pushed and shoved.
What did they expect to hear
As they pressed him into the hungry sea?
Water devours. Did they not know
He was the Word of God?
And you and me
For whom or what do we crave?
At whose table will we eat?
The sea and our boats are full of fish,
Yet he calls us to leave them
To the crowd
And one by one to follow him.
My empty, ravenous stomach growls
To argue with my head,
Surrounded by open, perishing beaks
Waiting to be fed.

25. Luke 19:1-10 Zacchaeus

Zacchaeus was small in stature
>But that wasn't his problem
>>But that was his problem
>>>Because he became a tax-collector to be Big in the eyes of his family and community.

His house was bigger, his mule was bigger, and as his possessions grew,
>His hunger grew bigger, his need grew bigger, his desire grew bigger.

Because Zacchaeus was small in stature,
>He climbed a tree to see,
>>But that wasn't his problem
>>But that was his problem because

Zacchaeus needed a new perspective, a new forgiveness, a new birth,
>And Jesus, because he was born from above, looked up and said,
>>"Come down, I am going to your house today."

Jesus looked up to see and he saw Zacchaeus' hunger
>And though it wasn't for food, Jesus ate with him,
>>For to eat at the table with Jesus means forgiveness,
>>>a new perspective, a new birth from above.

Then Zacchaeus gave away twice what he had taken
>For that was his problem,
>>But that wasn't his problem
>>For Jesus said,
>>>"Today salvation has come to this house."

That was Zacchaeus' problem
>And that is my problem
>>And the problem and work of the world.

26. John 15:1-13: "Remain in me, and I will remain in you. No branch can bear fruit by itself; it must remain in the vine."

There was once a vine with many branches. The branches were covered with rich, red, luscious fruit and the branches sang the praises of the vine for being the source of their fruit. With time, however, one of the branches began to wonder. "Why are we singing the praises of the vine? If it were not for us there would be no fruit. The vine without its branches would be bare." With time, the branch began to influence the others. "Why are you singing the praises of the vine? If it were not for us there would be no fruit. The vine without its branches would be bare. Perhaps we should bear our own fruit without the vine." The other branches began to wonder. It was true that sometimes they bore no fruit, that some seasons the vine seemed not to care nor hear their prayer. They wondered ... but they said, "Why should we doubt during the dry times, when we have experienced the vine's care in the good times?" So they waited. But the branch that doubted replaced his trust with pride and confidence in himself. "I will separate from the vine and they will see who bears the best fruit!" So he did. And with time, the proud and haughty branch shriveled up in the warm sunshine. Moral: There is no fruit without the vine.

27. Luke 4:18: The Spirit Of The Lord
And Jesus stood up to read,
"The Spirit of the Lord is upon me ..."
The child ran to the rabbi,
"The Messiah has come."
And the rabbi came to see.
But it was only Jesus of Nazareth
So the rabbi returned home.
Each Advent the Messiah comes
But still the poor are with us,
The imprisoned in their prison cells.
The disciples were wrong,
The apostles deceived,
The prophets, priests, and preachers
Wasted their breath,
Thy kingdom has not come.
Thy will is far from done.
Yet nevertheless we pray:
"Thine is the kingdom and the power and the glory,"

For women can vote,
And slaves no longer wear chains
Nor hide in underground tunnels,
Nor Christians in catacombs,
Lepers are loved,
And demons transformed,
And daughters freed from their fathers' vows[3]
And sisters from their brothers' lusts.[4]
We cry for a new coming
Unaware he is here —
Coming and going,
Crucified and resurrected daily.

28. Enactment of Matthew 5:38-41

Do not let your opponent dictate your defense. Do not mirror evil. Resist, even be creatively aggressive, but without violence. Be creative. Use your initiative.

A. Actors: the slave and the master.

Stand opposite each other. The master strikes the slave's right cheek with his right hand (it is a violation against the law to use the left hand). The slave turns his left cheek so the master can hit it, thus becoming equal. Therefore, you the victim can act as a human even in your slavery, your victimhood, thus bringing a new reality to the framework of the old domination system.

B. Indebtedness was the major social problem, the way the domination system kept control. If anyone sue you for your coat (outer garment, the robe that keeps you warm at night) give them your underclothes, as well. If loanee is poor, you shall give the coat back by sunset, so that your neighbor may sleep in the cloak (Deuteronomy 24:10-13). You may retrieve it the next morning, and so on.

Actors: judge, suer, poor. The suer has come to court to sue.
Suer: "He has not paid his debt."
Judge: "The suer is entitled to your coat."

Poor: "Here, and take this (socks) and this (shoes) and this (shirt) and ..."

(This enactment is more appropriate in a retreat setting.)

C. There was a Roman law that said a soldier could only ask the oppressed to carry their luggage for one mile. If more, they would be punished.

Actors: Roman soldier, slave, centurion.

Roman soldier: "Here, you, carry my bags."

Slave: "Sure, how are you? Been here long? Where are you going?"

Walk to road marker: one mile.

Roman soldier: "Stop! This is one mile."

Slave: "I have nothing else to do. I will go on."

Walk to road marker: one mile. Slave sees centurion.

Slave: "I have carried this bag for over a mile."

Centurion to Roman soldier: "You will be punished."

Roman soldier: "He said he wanted to."

Centurion: "You will receive ten lashes. It is the law."

(These three enactments are credited to Walter Wink, author of *Engaging the Powers*, experienced at a workshop by the same name, Well Spring, Texas, October 28, 1995.)

---

1. Short story by Hans Christian Andersen, "In the Uttermost Parts of the World."

2. Revised, Elaine M. Ward, *Children and Worship* (Prescott, AZ: Educational Ministries, 1993), p. 6.

3. Jephthah's Daughter: Judges 11.

4. Tamar and Amnon, David's son: 2 Samuel 13.

6

Litanies And Readings

The Psalms in our Bible are a hymnal, meant to be read or sung aloud. John 1 is also a hymn of praise, for Israel was a people of the "ear." The oral word was so important that its hearers experienced participation in the hearing, the words slipped down from the ear into the heart, stirring it to act, to "move the feet," into the slums, the prisons, the poverties of life, to accomplish what it was sent to do. The following litanies are "sent" for you "to do":

1. Choral Reading: John 1:1-18 (The following choral reading is designed to be read by seven or five readers and thus numbered.)
Reader 1: In the beginning was the Word,
Reader 2: and the Word was with God,
Readers 1 and 2: and the Word was God.
Reader 3: He was with God in the beginning.
Reader 4: All things came into being through him,
Reader 5: and without him not one thing came into being.
Reader 1 (or 6): In him was life,
Reader 2 (or 7): and the life was the light of all people.
All readers: The light shines in the darkness, and the darkness did not overcome it.
Reader 1: There was a man sent from God;
Reader 2: whose name was John.
Reader 3: He came as a witness to testify to the light,
Reader 4: so that all might believe through him.
Reader 5: He himself was not the light;
Reader 6: but he came to testify to the light.
Reader 7: The true light, which enlightens everyone, was coming into the world.

Reader 1: He was in the world,

Reader 2: and the world came into being through him,

Reader 3: yet the world did not know him.

Reader 4: He came to what was his own,

Reader 5: and his own people did not accept him.

Reader 6: But to all who received him,

Reader 7: who believed in his name,

Readers 1-7: he gave power to become children of God, who were born, not of blood or the will of the flesh or of the will of man, but of God.

2. A Litany of Confession:

Leader: Almighty God, we confess we have put our hope in things we could see and touch.

People: Send your Holy Spirit to open our eyes.

Leader: We have forgotten your presence in our lives.

People: Keep us alert!

Leader: We have been afraid to follow you, for this world tempts us with its power.

People: Keep us awake!

Leader: We have doubted and become discouraged about our lives, the world, and the church.

People: Send your Holy Spirit to fill us with your words so that we may endure as your faithful people to the end.

All: Amen.

3. A Litany of Thanksgiving:

Leader: For lack of love and for love,

People: We give you thanks, O Lord.

Leader: For hunger and for food,

People: We give you thanks, O Lord.

Leader: For your absence and for your ever-present presence,

People: We give you thanks, O Lord.

All: We ask you, O Lord, for all these things and thank you for all these things, for we know that in our lack and in our longing we more readily recognize our need and dependency upon you, the Giver of all good gifts. Amen.

4. A Litany of the Church:
In all time of our fear and doubt;
In all time of our possibility;
In the valley of the shadow of death;
And in the day of frustration,
And of fulfillment,
Hear us, dear Lord.

5. A Service of Worship for the Beginning of School:
Call to Worship: "Your word, O Lord, is a map to my feet and a light to my path" (Psalm 119:105). Come, let us worship the Lord.
Instrumental solo or group singing (children)
Processional of Bible during the singing of the following hymn. Children carry a variety of Bibles in different shapes and different colors of covers to place on the altar.
Hymn: "Thy Word Is A Lamp"
Litany of Thanksgiving:
Leader (a child): For a new beginning,
Congregation: We give you thanks, O Lord.
Leader: For books that give us information, wisdom, and thy will,
Congregation: We give you thanks, O Lord.
Leader: For teachers who help us discover the wonder of your world,
Congregation: We give you thanks, O Lord.
Leader: For eyes with which to see and read, ears to hear, and tongues to speak,
Congregation: We give you thanks, O Lord.
Leader: For a place where we may learn,
Congregation: We give you thanks, O Lord.
Leader: And for your Word, the Bible, and the Christ,
Congregation: We give you thanks, O Lord.
Scripture Reading: Proverbs 22:1-6

6. A Litany of Water:
Prelude: Recording of water sounds[1]
  (Project on screen a slide of a waterfall, running brook, ocean, glass of water, or use a video of water movement. Beside an empty

glass and a pitcher of water on the altar, share stories of places where people have nothing to drink. Pour the water into the glass. Use a microphone to magnify the sound of water, explaining how we can make a difference by digging new wells and pipelines through the money we share, and our prayers for water.)

Liturgist: Water.

Reader 1: "As the deer pants for streams of water,
so my soul pants for you, O God.
My soul thirsts for God, for the living God.
When can I go and meet with God?" (Psalm 42:1-2).

Reader 2: The pouring out of water makes gardens grow and deserts bloom. Without living water we dry up. We need the living water of the Word.

All: I will drink from the stream of living water, flowing from within.

Liturgist: Water.

Reader 1: "... Whoever is thirsty, let him come; and whoever wishes, let him take the free gift of the water of life" (Revelation 22:17b).

Reader 2: We long for more than physical water. We are thirsty, parched for the water of which Jesus spoke to the Samaritan woman at the well, the water of eternal life. When our lives are dry in the deserts through which we walk, we cry out for water in the wilderness. We long to experience Jesus' presence in our lives through prayer, for he is our water, the water without which we truly perish.

All: I will drink from the stream of living water, flowing from within.

Liturgist: Water.

Reader 1: "The voice is over the waters; the God of glory thunders, the Lord thunders over the mighty waters" (Psalm 29:3).

Reader 2: Water is the source of life, of cleansing, refreshment, healing, blessing, renewal. I am smoothed and energized by the gift of water.

All: I will drink from the stream of living water, flowing from within.

Liturgist: Water.

Reader 1: "On the last and greatest day of the Feast, Jesus stood and said in a loud voice, 'If a man is thirsty, let him come to me and drink. Whoever believes in me, as the scripture has said, streams of living water will flow from within him.' By this he meant the Spirit ..." (John 7:37-39).

Reader 2: "Because I have been athirst I will dig a well that others may drink." (Arabian proverb)

All: I will drink from the stream of living water, flowing from within.

Hymn: "God of the Sparrow"

(Add the verse: God of the rainbow, God of the sea, God of the watered land, How does the creature say Thanks, How does the creature say Please?

God of the Spirit, God of our Christ, God of the thirsty soul, How does the creature say Bless Animals, Babies, and Trees?)

Benediction: Go now in the name of God who gives us gifts of sunshine and water, and Jesus the Christ who is the living water, and the Holy Spirit who opens our throats to drink and to share. Amen.

7. Call to Worship: John 4:7-15

Readers: Narrator, Samaritan woman, Jesus

Narrator: A Samaritan woman came to draw water, and Jesus said to her,

Jesus: "Give me a drink."

Samaritan woman: "How is it that you, a Jew, ask a drink of me, a woman of Samaria?"

Narrator: Jews do not share things in common with Samaritans.

Jesus: "If you knew the gift of God, and who it is that is saying to you, 'Give me a drink,' you would have asked him, and he would have given you living water."

Samaritan woman: "Sir, you have no bucket, and the well is deep. Where do you get that living water? Are you greater than our ancestor Jacob, who gave us the well, and with his sons and his flocks drank from it?"

Jesus: "Everyone who drinks of this water will be thirsty again, but those who drink of the water that I will give them will never be thirsty. The water that I will give will become in them a spring of water gushing up to eternal life."

Samaritan woman: "Sir, give me this water, so that I may never be thirsty or have to keep coming here to draw water."

Narrator: Come, let us worship the one who gives living water.

Hymn: "Thank You, God, for Water, Soil, and Air" or "All Things Bright and Beautiful"

Prayer of Confession: We are thirsty, Lord, we long for living water, yet our throats are too narrow for water to enter and pass through. Open our throats and our hearts and our minds to Your living water so that we may share this water with all thirsty souls. In the name of Christ, who is that living water. Amen.

Words of Assurance: Jesus said, "Take drink. You are my beloved."

8. Choral Reading: "Jesus Walks On The Water" (John 6:16-29)

Chorus 1: When evening came, his disciples went down to the lake,

Chorus 2: where they got into a boat and set off across the lake for Capernaum.

Chorus 1: By now it was dark *(slowly and "deep")*

Solo 1: And Jesus had not yet joined them.

Chorus 2: A strong wind was blowing *(loud)*

Chorus 1: and the waters grew rough *(even louder).*

Chorus 1 and 2: When they had rowed three or three and a half miles

Solo 1: they saw Jesus approaching the boat

Chorus 2: walking on the water *(surprised)*

Chorus 1: and they were terrified *(with fear).*

Solo 1: But he said to them,

Solo 2: "It is I; do not be afraid," *(calmly).*

Chorus 2: Then they were willing to take him into the boat,

Chorus 1: and immediately

Chorus 2: the boat reached the shore where they were heading.

Chorus 1 and 2: The next day

Chorus 1: the crowd that had stayed on the opposite shore of the lake

Chorus 2: realized that only one boat had been there
Solo 1: and that Jesus had not entered it with his disciples ...
Chorus 1: When they found him on the other side of the lake, they asked
Solo 1: "Rabbi, when did you get here?"
Chorus 1: Jesus answered,
Solo 2: "I tell you the truth, you are looking for me, not because you saw miraculous signs but because you ate the loaves and had your fill. Do not work for food that spoils, but for food that endures to eternal life, which the Son of Man will give you. On him God the Father has placed his seal of approval."
Chorus 1: Then they asked him,
Chorus 2: "What must we do to do the works God requires?"
Solo 1: Jesus answered,
Solo 2: "The work of God is this: to believe in the one he has sent."

9. "In Those Days" (Mark 10:27; 13:7-8; 24-25)
Leader: There will be wars and rumors of wars
People: But for God all things are possible.
Leader: There will be famine and there will be earthquakes
People: But for God all things are possible.
Leader: The sun will be darkened and the moon will not give its light
People: But for God all things are possible.
Leader: The stars will fall from heaven and the powers in the heavens will be shaken
People: But for God all things are possible. Amen.

10. A Litany of Joy:
Leader: "I was glad when they said to me, 'Let us go to the house of the Lord.' " Show me what you do when you are glad and use that as your refrain.
People: *Clap, smile, sing, make movement, and so forth.*
Leader: "Make a joyful noise to God."
People: *Clap, etc.*
Leader: "Make a joyful noise to God for those who teach or heal."
People: *Clap, etc.*

83

Leader: "Make a joyful noise to God for those who visit the sick or feed the hungry or house the homeless or pray for those in need."
People: *Clap, etc.*
Leader: "Make a joyful noise to God for all those who love one another."
People: *Clap, etc.*
Leader: "Make a joyful noise to God, for we are God's people and give God praise!"

11. A Litany of Creation:

First Reader: "In the beginning God created the heavens and the earth."
All: And it was good!
Second Reader: But the water is polluted, the sea creatures destroyed, the land filled with slums and highways and nuclear waste.
All: It is not good!
Third Reader: God created women and men in God's own image, giving them power to create and have compassion for all creation.
All: And it was good!
Fourth Reader: But we have used the earth as our source of supply and our power to compete and excel, argue and lie, make weapons and destroy.
All: It is not good!
First Reader: We should laugh and live for today.
Second Reader: We should cry and die for tomorrow.
Third Reader: We will find a way.
Fourth Reader: We will reap sorrow.
Fifth Reader: Do not lose your laughter in despair, nor your hope in grief. Evil exists and so does love. Work for peace and a better world. For our Lord was a suffering and a joyous servant.
All: In Christ's name, forgive us and give us new life. Amen.

12. A Litany of Assurance:

Leader: God is with us as we grow physically.
People: God is the Power and the Wisdom and the Presence that persuades us to grow.

Leader: God is with us as we grow emotionally from caring for our own self-centered needs to compassion for the needs of others.
People: God is the Power and the Wisdom and the Presence that persuades us to grow.
Leader: God is with us as we grow mentally toward fuller understanding of ourselves, of others, and of the world.
People: God is the Power and the Wisdom and the Presence that persuades us to grow.
Leader: God is with us as we grow spiritually in our relationships, our insights, and in our faithfulness.
People: God is the Power and the Wisdom and the Presence that persuades us to grow with faith and hope and joy.

13. A Litany of Thanksgiving: *(in unison)*
For the things we take for granted:
A good night's sleep,
An awakening kiss,
The smell of rain renewing earth,
Another day,
For these and all unmentioned things we pray.
For things unseen:
The joy of friends and family,
The peace as soft as fallen snow,
The hope beyond all impossibility,
Believing lengthened into knowing,
The power of the Holy Spirit's way,
For these and all unseen things we pray,
And now we pray together the prayer Christ taught us: The Lord's Prayer.

14. Leader: Blow the Spirit of your word upon us, O God,
People: So that we may be transformed by the renewing of our minds.
Leader: May the breath of your Spirit give voice to the silent, freedom to the captive, food to the hungry, and transformation to those who are of this world.

People: Be with us through our fruitless seasons, Lord, and our separations from one another, and shake our conformances to the world, as we rejoice in our differences through the unity of Christ.

15. Leader: God created us to seek God.
People: Come, Holy Spirit, come.
Leader: Our yearning for God gives us meaning and direction and is our most precious treasure.
People: Come, Holy Spirit, come.
Leader: For we are more than conquerors through him who loves us.
All: Come, Holy Spirit, come!

16. Headline Litany for Aug. 29-Sept. 3, 1989[2]
Speaker: Two Marines die in shelling in Beiruit battle.
People: God, give us peace.
Speaker: Boxer hospitalized after knockout.
People: God, give us peace.
Speaker: One dead, 23 hurt in prison riot.
People: God, give us peace.
Speaker: Hijackers set new deadline.
People: God, give us peace.
Speaker: Man charged with raping pregnant woman.
People: God, give us peace.
Speaker: Manila says Aquino was killed by hit man.
People: God, give us peace.
Speaker: Child murderer executed today.
People: God, give us peace.
Speaker: Lebanon troops on alert after massacre.
People: God, give us peace.
Speaker: Obituaries: *(local names)*
All: God, give us peace.

17. Leader: "Can these bones come back to life?" Can these bones of exiled children, women, men, these refugees and all homeless persons inside and outside their homeland, come back to life?
All: Sovereign Lord, only you can answer that!

Leader: Can the bones of the Holocaust victims, their descendants, and all who have inherited the same inhuman treatment come back to life?

All: Sovereign Lord, only you can answer that!

Leader: Can the bones of the abused and rejected children and women come back to life?

All: Sovereign Lord, only you can answer that!

Leader: Can all those who feel unheard and abandoned by a silent God come back to life?

All: Sovereign Lord, only you can answer that!

Leader: Can we with bones and blood, skin and sinew, muscle and membrane come back to life?

All: With God all things are possible.

Prayer of the Pastor, the People, and The Lord's Prayer: Wind, blow mightily into this place and into each body here. Bring life to our dry bones. Fill us with Your breath so that we may speak hope wherever there is dryness and death, and all may know that You are Lord. (Ezekiel 37:1-15)

18. A Litany for Justice: *(Read aloud Matthew 12:17-32. Ask the group to read the indented material.)*

Where there is oppression
   Let the prophets arise and speak.
Where there is failure
   Let there be faith.
Where there is hatred
   Let there be harmony.
Where there is fear
   Let there be love.
Where there is violence
   Let there be peace.
Where there is suffering
   Let there be healing.
Where there is bondage
   Let there be freedom.
Where there is silence
   Let there be speech.

Wherever there is struggle for justice
    Let there be servants of a just God.
    Let there be me and let there be you and let us be one. Amen.

19. A Litany of Reconciliation:
Leader: Across the barriers that divide race from race:
All: Reconcile us, O Christ, by your cross.
Leader: Across the barriers that divide the rich from the poor:
All: Reconcile us, O Christ, by your cross.
Leader: Across the barriers that divide people of different faiths:
All: Reconcile us, O Christ, by your cross.
Leader: Across the barriers that divide men and women, young and old:
All: Reconcile us, O Christ, by your cross. Teach us to grow in unity with all of your creatures, O God. Amen.

20. Pass the Peace: Hug, smile, and bless your neighbor, as you pass the peace in the name of Christ.

21. A Litany of Looking:
Leader: Great Creator, God of all, we thank You for the amazing gift of eyes and of seeing.
People: Blessed are the eyes that see what we see ...
Leader: We thank you, God, for the gifts of pictures and books, flowers and brooks, for the things You have created for us to see and the things we have created, made in Your image.
People: Blessed are the eyes that see what we see ...
Leader: We thank You, our heavenly Parent, for the people and places we love and can see, and for the gift of insight, seeing with the eye of the spirit.
People: Blessed are the eyes that see what we see ...
Leader: We thank You for Jesus who saw what we cannot see and showed us, by healing our sight, a new vision of Your kingdom here on earth.
People: Blessed are the eyes that see what we see ...
Leader: Help us to regain the wonder of sight and teach us to see the beauty You have prepared in every aspect of our lives, to be

awake so that we may pray with our eyes, as well as our words and our hearts.

All: In Christ's name and sight. Amen.

22. A Litany for Advent:
Leader: *(softly)* Someone is coming.
People: *(softly)* **I hope he's a king.**
Leader: *(build in volume)* Someone is coming.
People: *(build volume, as leader)* **I hope he's a savior.**
Leader: Someone is coming.
People: Perhaps he's a soldier.
Leader: Someone is coming.
People: He must be the Messiah.
Leader: It's only a baby.
People: Who grew to be a Servant.
All: *(boldly)* **His name is Emmanuel, who is our Savior, Lord, and King.**

23. A Litany of Celebration:
Leader: God is our refuge and strength,
a very present help in trouble.
Voices from congregation or one voice: In South Africa? In El Salvador? In the Middle East? *(and so forth)* **In this place?**
Leader: We will not fear, though the earth should change,
though the mountains shake in the heart of the sea;
though its waters roar and foam,
though the mountains tremble with its tumult.
Response: Though the fish die in polluted waters and children's lungs are filled with polluted air? Though the trees are destroyed and the land laid barren? *(and so forth)*
Leader: There is a river whose streams make glad the city of God,
the holy habitation of the Most High.
God is in the midst of the city; it shall not be moved;
God will help it when the morning dawns.
Response: A clean stream? A happy city? A new Jerusalem? Another dawn? But the nations are in an uproar, the kingdoms totter; he utters his voice, the earth melts.

Leader: Come, behold the works of the Lord;
see the desolations he has brought on the earth.
**Response: God makes wars cease to the end of the earth;
God breaks the bow, and shatters the spear;
God burns the shields with fire.**
Leader: "Be still, and know that I am God! *(silence)*
I am exalted among the nations,
I am exalted in the earth."
**All: The Lord of hosts is with us;
the God of Jacob is our refuge.**

24. Jesus said in John 14:1-14: "I am going to the Father!"

Leader: "Do not let your hearts be troubled.
Trust in God; trust also in me. I am going...."
**Chorus: Where are you going? Where have you been?
Why are you leaving? Will you come back again?**
Leader: "And if I go and prepare a place for you, I will come back. I will come back and take you to be with me that you also may be where I am...."
Chorus: *Repeat refrain from above.*
Leader: "I am the way and the truth and the life.
If you really knew me,
you would know my Father as well...."
Chorus: *Repeat refrain from above.*
Leader: "I will do whatever you ask in my name,
so that the Son may bring glory to the Father.
I am going to the Father...."
Chorus: *Repeat refrain from above.*

25. Harvest Reading:

Reader: Listen, my children, and give heed.
Chorus, congregation, or single reader: We are not children!
Reader: Jesus said, "Unless you become as little children, you will not enter the kingdom of God."
"A sower set out to sow his seed on a warm and sunny day."
Chorus: We don't do that anymore. We have machines to do our work.

Reader: What shall it profit you if you gain the whole world and lose your soul? "Packing his sack with seeds to sow, the sower threw out his seeds to grow and some fell along the way."

Chorus: Where will we find our way?

Reader: "Hungry birds eager for their feed flew down to devour every seed, 'til the path was smooth and bare."

Chorus: We are hungry. Where will we find our food?

Reader: "Some of the seed fell on a stone and shriveled up when the warm sun shone, so no one knew they were there."

Chorus: Where are we? We are a rootless, restless people. Where will we find our roots?

Reader: "Those that fell in the thorns and weeds were choked and destroyed ..."

Chorus: The weeds of drug and drink, desperation and doubt, choke and destroy our hope and our joy.

Reader: "But the seeds that fell in the wet, rich ground grew from the sunshine and the rain into the ripened golden grain, filling fields for miles around."

Chorus: Where is our rich soil, sunshine and rain that will feed and nourish us?

Reader: "Those who have ears then let them hear."

Chorus: For such is the love of God, life and growth in a tiny seed.

Reader and Chorus: We marvel at the wonder of Your world and love, Lord, charged with grandeur, "seared with trade and smeared with toil. For there lives the dearest freshness deep down things ... Because the Holy Ghost over the bent World broods with warm breast and with ah! bright wings."[3]

26. A Litany of Praise:

Leader: Praise God for all we lose.

Congregation: I will let go!

Leader: Praise God for lost innocence so we may be one.

Congregation: I will let go!

Leader: Praise God for silence that welcomes us to hear and then to speak.

Congregation: I will let go!

91

Leader: Praise God for death so we will see the beauty of now.

Congregation: I will let go!

Leader: What's lost is nothing to what's found, for out of the ending comes the new beginning.

Congregation and Leader: Praise God! Amen.

27. A Litany of Petition:

Leader: Jesus Christ was born a baby in a stable ...

People: "It matters nothing if one is born in a duck yard, if one has only lain in a swan's egg."

Leader: "And the child grew and became strong; he was filled with wisdom, and the grace of God was upon him" (Luke 2:40).

People: May God's grace be upon us all as we grow in wisdom and strength through Jesus, our Christ.

28. A Reading: "Give Me A Sign" Thomas said, "Unless I see the mark of the nails in his hands and put my finger in the mark of the nails, I will not believe" (John 20:19-20).

Reader: Easter is a sign for two doors.

Chorus: One says, "Exit," the other, "Enter."

Reader: Easter is a time of signs.

Chorus: Give us a sign.

Man: "Unless I see the mark of the nails in his hands and put my finger in the mark of the nails, I will not believe" (John 20:19-20).

Reader: The evangelist John, writing his story of Jesus, concluded: "Now Jesus did many other signs in the presence of his disciples."

Chorus: We need our signs. Give us a sign.

Reader: The disciples on their way to Emmaus did not recognize the stranger who walked with them, but invited him to stay. When he was at the table with them, he took bread, blessed it and broke it, and gave it to them. Then their eyes were opened, and they recognized him in the sign in the broken bread (Luke 24:13-31).

Chorus: Give us a sign.

Woman: My name is B.G. and I am a clown. It is my first time to be in clown ministry without my husband "Happy Jack" and I am frightened. My husband's vocation is a clown. Over and over he asked me to join him, but I had always refused. "Lord, send me a sign!" I prayed.

One day he was clowning for the handicapped children who clapped and cheered and loved every moment of his silly, silent antics. One of the children saw me watching and took my hand, and looking up into my eyes said, "He make me feel good. I love Happy Jack."

The child's eyes were shining. He had received a gift, the gift of love and joy in the humor of the clown. Now he was sharing that gift with her. "You know what he need?" he continued.

"No," I asked curiously, for I did not know.

The child replied, "He need a little clown."

Chorus: God, send us a sign!

Woman: As I drove into the parking lot in my makeup and costume that morning, a car full of camp girls saw me, giggled and waved. Driving past, one of the girls stuck her head and arms out of the car window. Turning toward the clown she smiled and with her fingers made the sign of "Yeah! Go with it! Okay!"

Chorus: Lord, send us a sign.

Reader: Jesus gave us the sign of love: "If you love me, you will keep my commandments," he said to his friends.

Reader 1: "... I am the door," Jesus said. "Whoever enters by me will be saved ..." (John 10:9a).

Reader 2: "When they (Paul and Barnabas) arrived (in Antioch), they called the church together and related all that God had done with them, and how he had opened a door of faith for the Gentiles" (Acts 14:27).

Reader 1: "I have set before you an open door, which no one is able to shut" (Revelation 3:8).

Reader 2: "Listen! I am standing at the door, knocking; if you hear my voice and open the door, I will come in to you and eat with you, and you with me" (Revelation 3:20).

Reader 1: "After this I looked and there in heaven a door stood open!" (Revelation 4:1).

Chorus: Lord, give us a sign.

Reader 2: Aslan (the Great Lion that represented Christ to the animals of Narnia) approached the Door and shouted "TIME" and the Door flew open, as Aslan called the stars home. The creatures rushing toward Aslan looked at him, and on some faces there appeared fear and hatred and they swerved to his left into his huge black shadow. But those who looked in the face of Aslan and loved him, though frightened at the same time, came in at the Door on Aslan's right. "Peter, High King of Narnia," said Aslan. "Shut the Door." The children looked around and found themselves in warm daylight, the blue sky above them, flowers at their feet, and laughter in Aslan's eyes. "Come further in! Come further up!" he shouted over his shoulder. Peter, shivering with cold, leaned out into the darkness and pulled the Door to ... and locked it. They had seen strange things enough through that Doorway. "Come further in! Come further up!" Aslan shouted over his shoulder. Then Aslan and his friends with great joy walked hand in hand to that land across the sea they called "home."[4]

Reader 1: Easter is a sign for two doors. One says, "Exit," the other "Enter," the "exit" of Death and the "entrance" of Christ and new life.

Chorus: Thank you, Lord, for your signs! Amen.

29. John 1:35-42 Welcoming Strangers: *(role play or use puppets)*

John: Hello, I am John the Baptist in this play.

Andrew, a Disciple: I am a disciple of John the Baptist.

2nd disciple: I am a disciple, too. Who are you? *(to audience)*

John: Stick to the story!

2nd disciple: Sorry!

Andrew: Are we ready to begin?

John: I think so. Where is Jesus?

Jesus: Here I am!

John: *(To disciples)* Look, the Lamb of God.

Disciples: *(Looking around, puzzled)* Lamb? Lamb? I do not see a lamb!

John: I am speaking of Jesus.

Disciples: *(together)* Oh, I see now! Let us follow him!

Jesus: What do you want?

Disciples: Rabbi, where are you staying?

Jesus: Come and you will see.

Narrator: They spent that day with him.

Andrew: Simon! Simon! We have been with Jesus, bar Joseph. We have found the Christ!

Simon: Take me to him!

Narrator: Then Andrew, Simon's brother, brought Simon to Jesus.

Jesus: You are Simon son of John. You will be called "Cephas."

Simon: My Lord! *(Turns to Andrew)* What does "Cephas" mean?

Andrew: "It means "rock."

Simon: Rock? Rock in my head? Rock and roll? Rock-a-bye baby?

All: Peter!

30. The blessing of the "beasts" and children: Having asked the children to bring their favorite teddy bear or other stuffed animal or toy friend, invite them to come forward.

"... In Christ God was reconciling the world to himself ..." (2 Corinthians 5:19).

The large South African church was packed with people. The North American professor was expected but unexpectedly delayed. When he at last arrived, he was immediately escorted to the first row and when the minister saw him, he substituted English in order to include his guests. Children were mixed among the congregation, and when the benediction had been given the minister said, "Amen!" which means "the end. So be it." Then the minister said, "Let the children come!" The children came to the altar area. They came by twos and threes and fours. They packed the aisles. There must have been forty or fifty or sixty children seated on the floor, crowding the chancel area, lifting their eager faces as the ministers walked among them, placing their hands on the children's heads and shoulders, cupping their cheeks, and blessing them, saying, "Your name is written on the palm of God's hand." When the preacher had passed among them all, he again spoke to the awaiting congregation. "There is nothing more important for these children than to know that Jesus loves each one of them personally, that their names are written on the palm of his hand, for God knows and loves each one of you by name."

Leader: *(To congregation)* In a day of violence, child abuse, and hunger, living in a land that exalts power, prestige, and production, children need the assurance of their favorite cuddly friends. We do well to take time to bless the children and their friends.

(To children) We have come together at this time to receive God's blessing. God was in Jesus, hugging us. We love because God first loves us.

Today we are blessing the friends we love. To bless means to be there for the other. "I will be with you" is God's blessing.

Blessing: In the name of God who is Love, I bless you with God's love. *(Bless the children. Walk among the children and "bless" them, saying)* Your name is written on the palm of God's hand.

(To children) Now I invite you to say these words with me as you bless the friend you have brought with you. Let us say the words together: *(children and leader)* "God bless you. Amen."

31. John 8:1-11: In Crisis Times

Crowd: My hands gripped the heavy stone in each hand, eager to let them fly, for my target was she who had disobeyed the Law. If she got away with it, where would it end?

My action will be a model for my children, but why are my knees shaking, my mouth dry, my nails digging into the impenetrable rock? Who is this woman? Who is this man?

Woman: My face lies upon this rocky land, my fate is in their hands, heavy with stones, my knees are shaking, my mouth is dry, my nails dig into these stones that can kill. Who is this man?

Jesus: Who is this woman? Who are these people so eager to destroy life and honor death? My knees are shaking, my mouth is dry, my nails dig pictures in the dirt, for they are testing me.

The Law is clear. The scriptures say: "... you shall stone that ... woman to death with stones; the men of her city shall stone her to death with stones" (cf. Deuteronomy 17:5; 22:21).

What would you have me do?

Me/You: My knees are shaking, my mouth is dry, my nails dig into my perceptions, illusion, beliefs by which I live. My ears are filled with story and so are my eyes. My noise intuits my intrigue, for is this not my story?

Who am I? Who is this crowd: Who is this woman? Who is this man? With whom will I identify?

"You search the scriptures, because you think that in them you have eternal life; and it is they that bear witness to me; yet you refuse to come to me that you may have life" (John 5:39-40).

"Let the one among you who is without sin cast the first stone ... And you, go and sin no more."

32. A Litany of Love:

One: For the creation of the world, night and day, sun and rain,
All: We give you our love and thanks.
One: For land and sea, flower, bird, and bee,
All: We give you our love and thanks.
One: For life and food from seed and tree,
All: We give you our love and thanks.
One: For love of friends and family,
All: We give you our love and thanks.
One: For the birth of Christ your Son,
All: We give you our love and thanks.
One: For your everlasting love,
All: We give you our love and thanks.

33. "Why Do You Go To Church?"

When Lauren, my seven-year-old granddaughter, got into the car, I handed her a small, new teddy bear. "Where did you get this, Granny?" "I am going to preach at a church for 'Teddy Bear Sunday' and they are giving the children these bears. I want to give mine to you." Lauren hugged the small teddy bear and was silent. Then she said, "Granny, why do you go to church?" "I believe there is a Force whom we call God that created this beautiful creation, loves us, and lures us into loving. I go to thank and praise God." Since Lauren was still listening, I continued. "I also go to be with the people there who are passionately interested in what interests me." She continued to listen. This was unusual for my talkative granddaughter! Since I was being honest, I added, "I go to support the minister and his work because he is my friend. And Jesus is my friend."

A child wondered, "Why do I have to go to church?" One day he asked his father and his father replied, "I would rather fly with a pilot who has had lessons than with one who has not. I would rather learn about the Christian faith from a fellow Christian than from 'the one in the street.' "

Leader: What do you get at church?

Reader 1: *(a child from the congregation, standing)* At church I get acquainted with the man called Jesus who loves children and invites them to sit on his lap and talk with him in their imagination.

Reader 2: *(male)* I get spiritual food from prayer and the sacred story that forms and feeds and transforms my trust in God, my hope and love and courage in singing the church's sacred song.

Reader 3: *(female)* I get hands and hugs from the people in this church because we are the church together.

Leader: When you come to church, what do you get? *(Invite the congregation at large to spontaneously tell what they "get at church.")*

Reader 4: I get a place where we can praise and thank God for the Light, the Book, and the Body of Christ, the church.

Preacher: Let the people say, "Amen."

People: Amen!

34. Leader: Praise the name of God who led us out of bondage in Egypt.

People: Who led us out of bondage in _____ *(name your city or invite participants to name the city in which they were born).*

Leader: Forgive us our part in the bondage of others.

People: The bondage of slavery.

Leader: The bondage of unforgiveness and anger.

People: The bondage of complacency.

Leader: The bondage of prejudice.

People: The bondage of competition.

Leader: Help us recover a sense of faith and trust.

People: Of compassion and connection.

Leader: Of safety and strength.

People: Of identity.

Leader: Of integrity.

People: Of abundance.
Leader: And possibility.
All: Praise the Lord!

35. Leader: Praise God for all creation.
People: For artists: the ability to paint and draw and appreciate.
Leader: For musicians: The ability to sing and make music, to listen and enjoy.
People: For writers and teachers: the ability to speak and write words.
Leader: For actors and dancers: the ability to pretend and to move.
People: For dreamers: the ability to envision and hope.
Leader: For doctors and nurses: the ability to heal.
People: For lawyers and police, civil and private servants: the ability to help.
Leader: For mothers and fathers, children and families: the ability to nurture.
All: Praise God for all possibility: the ability to be a channel for God's creativity and love. Amen.

36. A Litany Of Healing (Luke 13:10-13):
Leader: Now Jesus was teaching in one of the synagogues on the sabbath.
Reader 1: And just then there appeared
Reader 2: a woman
Reader 3: with a spirit that had crippled her
Reader 4: for eighteen years.
Reader 1: She was bent over
Reader 2: and quite unable to stand up straight.
Leader: When Jesus saw her, he called her over and said,
Reader 1: "Woman, you are set free from your ailment."
Reader 2: When he laid hands on her
Reader 3: immediately
Reader 4: she stood up straight
All: and began praising God.
Leader: What spirit of weakness cripples you?

Reader 1: O, woman?

Reader 2: O, man?

Reader 3: What causes your bent-overness?

Reader 4: What will set you free?

Leader: Who or what tells you

Reader 1: "NO!"?

Reader 2: Calls you into the equality?

Reader 3: Names you a "daughter of Abraham"?

Reader 4: Releases and empowers you?

(Silence for reflection.)

Leader: You are set free from your ailment.

Leader: "There is merely bad luck in not being loved";

People: "There is tragedy in not loving."

Leader: "All of us, today, are dying of this tragedy."

People: "For violence and hatred dry up the heart itself";

Leader: "The long fight for justice exhausts the love that nevertheless gave birth to it."

All: "In the clamor in which we live, love is impossible and justice does not suffice."[5]

Benediction: Go now in the name of God who transforms our spirit of weakness and Jesus Christ, God's agent of healing, and the Holy Spirit who empowers us to be bold and to be whole. Amen.

---

1. *Dawn & Dusk by a Mountain Stream*, Richard Hooper, Recordist (Friday Harbor, WA: World Disc Productions, 1993).

2. Choose your own from current headlines. From Steven E. Burt, "Breathe Life Into Those Litanies," *Church Worship,* Dec. 1990 (Brea, CA: Educational Ministries).

3. *The Poems of Gerard Manley Hopkins,* W.H. Gerdner and N.H. MacKenzie, ed. (New York: Oxford University Press, 1979), p. 66.

4. C.S. Lewis, *The Last Battle* (New York: Collier), p. 143.

5. Walter Wink, *Engaging the Powers* (Minneapolis: Fortress Press, 1992), p. 399, from poster by Camus.

7

Offerings

"Think of us in this way, as servants of Christ and stewards of God's mysteries" (1 Corinthians 4:1).

We talk "softly" concerning the offering. A city missionary was giving a financial report, telling the needs of the youth in his district. Mark Twain said that he was so moved he could hardly wait for the preacher to finish. He fished $500 out of his wallet and was anxious to donate it to the cause. The preacher continued and as he went on and on, Twain's enthusiasm dwindled. It went down, he said, at $100 a clip until finally, when the collection plates were passed, Twain stole a dollar from one of them.

Yet God is the Creator and the Owner. All that we own, we owe. We are stewards created in the image of God. We are God's stewards.

Only as we know and experience the reality of God as Creator and Owner can we know that our ultimate purpose is to love and serve the God who loves us and who owns all things in this universe. Then we are motivated to be the faithful stewards that God wants us to be.

1. Rabbi Nahmann, hearing a foolish prayer at the close of the Day of Atonement, spoke to the man, saying, "I know that on the Eve of Atonement you prayed for 1,000 rubles all at once so that business would not disturb you from prayer. On the morning, knowing that much money would tempt you to begin a new business and have therefore even less time to pray, you asked for one half of the amount every half year, but before the gates closed, you changed your prayer to quarterly installments in order to learn and pray without being disturbed. But what makes you think your prayer is needed in heaven? Perhaps it is your gift that is needed instead."

101

2. More than anything else in the whole world, a man wanted to possess a house of his own. Not just any house, but a house that everyone would marvel at. So he worked long hours and hard days over many years until at last he acquired the house of his dreams.

Alas, once he set foot in his house, he was never seen again. He dared not leave his prize for fear that thieves would steal or vandals ruin what he had labored so hard to possess. Is it possible that whatever you possess, possesses you?

3. Offertory: All that we have is thine, O Lord, a trust from You. Let us now offer our gifts as a sign of our trust in God.

4. The rabbi said, "There is a full-fed zaddik." His disciples asked him what he meant by this. "Well," he explained, "one man buys himself a loaf of bread and eats it and another shares his bread with others."

5. "And what does the Lord require of you?
To act justly and to love mercy
and to walk humbly with your God" (Micah 6:8).

6. The apostle Paul referred to himself as being a worthless jar until he was filled with Christ. Jars are designed not only for filling but for pouring as well. They are meant to stand in a circle and receive from tipping the contents from one jar into another. This is the reason for community.

There are two kinds of jars (people), those who say, "No thanks, I've got plenty," and those who say, "I've got something here that can be shared. How can I get the courage to pour myself out?"[1]

7. If I were ever arrested for being a Christian, would there be enough evidence to convict me? All that we have, all that we are, we give to God, who has given us our all.

8. To bless another is to give a part of oneself, to "lean forward," to be there for the other, but it is only the divine blessing that enables us to bless. A good man asked God to grant him one wish.

The man requested that he would like to do good without knowing it. The wish was granted. Then with great wisdom God thought that it was such a good idea he would grant that wish to all persons. And so it was. Let us bless now with our offerings.

9. Once there was a farmer who owned a large field of corn. He seeded and weeded it carefully, for when it grew and he sold it, he would buy food for his family. No matter how hard he worked, however, the corn only withered and drooped, for there was no rain. "What will I do?" moaned the farmer, looking up at the sky and praying for rain. Two raindrops heard the farmer and one of them said, "I feel sorry for the farmer. His corn is drying up and dying. I wish I could help him." "You are only a small raindrop. What can you do?" "I cannot do much, it is true, but I can do what I can do. Here I go." The first raindrop began to fall as the second said, "If you insist upon going, I will go, too. Here I come!" The other raindrops gathered to see what was happening. "Let us go, too!" they cried together. One after one the raindrops fell on the farmer's corn and the corn grew and ripened, because one small raindrop tried to do what it could.

10. Blessed are the generous for they shall receive God's gifts.

11. All good gifts come from God. "And God is able to provide you with every blessing in abundance, so that you may always have enough of everything and may provide an abundance for every good work" (2 Corinthians 9:8).

12. "Thanks be to God for his inexpressible gift!" Who we are is God's gift to us. Who we become is our gift to God. Let us offer our gifts to God.

13. Mokusen Hiki was living in a temple in the province of Tamba. One of his adherents complained of the stinginess of his wife. Mokusen visited the adherent's wife and showed her his clenched fist before her face. "What do you mean by that?" asked the surprised woman. "Suppose my fist were always like that. What would you call it?" he asked. "Deformed," replied the woman. Then he opened his hand flat in her face and asked: "Suppose it were always like that. What then?" "Another kind of deformity," said the wife. "If you understand that much," finished Mokusen, "you are a good wife." Then he left. After his visit, this wife helped her husband to distribute as well as to save.[2] Let us give now what we have saved for others.

14. All that we own, we owe. Let us share together.

15. A Protestant minister, a Catholic priest, and a Jewish rabbi were discussing how much of the congregation's contributions they returned to God. The Protestant minister said, "I draw a line and throw up the money. What lands on this side belongs to the Lord." The Catholic priest said, "I draw a circle and stand inside and throw up the money. What lands inside the circle belongs to God." The Jewish rabbi said, "I draw a circle, too, and stand inside and throw up the money and say, "God, you take what you want first and the rest belongs to me."

God loves a cheerful giver.

16. "I believe it! 'Tis Thou, God, that givest, 'tis I who receive." Take now these gifts we bring in gratitude for the gift of faith.

17. When angry, the first thing we kick is the offering plate. As a family of faith we need to be more hospitable.

18. The sannyasi had reached the outskirts of the village and settled down under a tree for the night when a villager came running up to him and said, "The stone! The stone! Give me the precious stone!" "What stone?" asked the sannyasi. "Last night the Lord Shiva appeared to me in a dream," said the villager, "and told me that if I went to the outskirts of the village at dusk I should find a sannyasi who would give me a precious stone that would make me rich forever." The sannyasi rummaged in his bag and pulled out a stone. "He probably meant this one," he said, as he handed the stone over to the villager. "I found it on a forest path some days ago. You can certainly have it." The man gazed at the stone in wonder. It was a diamond, probably the largest diamond in the whole world, for it was as large as a person's head. He took the diamond and walked away. All night he tossed about in bed, unable to sleep. Next day at the crack of dawn he woke the sannyasi and said, "Give me the wealth that makes it possible for you to give this diamond away so easily."[3] May we willingly give of the wealth of our wisdom.

The following are two suggested ways of introducing stewardship.

1. "Stewardship" is a word that conjures up all sorts of images in our imagination and all sorts of emotions as well. Sometimes we talk about it too much. The other side of "the coin" is that we talk too little. I borrow from Robert Fulghum.[4]

Without going into all the details, Fulghum had a neighbor, a businessman who each morning rushed out of the house carrying a golf bag, gym bag, lunch bag, raincoat, umbrella, coffee cup, a sack of garbage for the dumpster, and his briefcase. The briefcase was pure, unblemished leather, with combination lock, and so forth. He drove a fast, well-built, new Range Rover.

The scene: man rushing to fast car, coffee cup in one hand, heavy briefcase in the other. The man places same on roof of his car, unlocks door, leaps into front seat, races motor, and makes a dash for his telephone as he backs out of his driveway.

Characters: man above, social worker for Episcopal church, and Fulghum.

Plot: Woman in old beat-up Ford sees cup and briefcase on roof. Honks to get driver's attention. No go. Fulghum also sees and honks. Businessman angry. Horns continue to honk. Businessman throws phone to floor, steps out of car irate, coffee cup slides off roof onto vest, bounces across hood, smashes into street, followed by briefcase, scraping its way across the hood, landing on top of broken coffee cup. Mission lady drives past with bright, "Have a nice day!" No, she does not run over the briefcase. Fulghum does.

The neighbor was furious, of course. It cost him money and time, and that is exactly what we are talking about, profit and loss.

And the verse (borrowed from Fulghum, who borrowed from the Bible, which borrowed from Jesus):

"What does it profit a man (or a woman — we have the same problem) if he (she) gains the whole world and loses his (her) own soul?"

2. "The Parable of the Lighthouse"[5]

The two men stood on the high cliffs. "What do you think, John?"

The other man listened to the night and answered: "With the wind pounding the waves against those rocks, it's hard to tell. But I'm afraid we have another one."

The first man shook his head: "Aye, and it's the third shipwreck this month. I'd best tell the crew."

He ran down the beach to a small lighthouse and pounded on the door: "Time to be moving! There's a wreck up near the north cliffs. We heard the cries in the wind."

The lifesaving crew tumbled out of the lighthouse, their sea-worn faces pale in the lantern-light. They plunged their little boats into the waves with amazing skill.

Such tragedies often struck that lonely coastline. A sudden shift in the winds, a thick fog rolling across the water, a treacherous turn in the tides — and an unlucky ship would slam into the sharp reefs, its hull slashed by the rocks. The cry would go out: "Abandon ship!"

But no sooner had these words left the captain's lips than the lantern of a lifesaving boat would appear in the darkness, leading the wrecked seamen to safety.

The little lighthouse soon grew famous. Each day, it seemed, there came a new knock on the door: "I've come to help!" "You saved my son's life. Please take this small sum, a sign of my gratitude." "I want to be part of your crew!"

The ramshackle buildings were repaired. Large boats were built and crew members traveled to schools for professional training.

Then one day, the entire crew sat in a circle on the sandy beach and held a meeting. A young man stood up and said: "What are we waiting for? Everyone knows that this old lighthouse isn't meeting our needs! We need bigger and better facilities!"

Everyone shook his head in agreement. Soon the old structure had been torn down and a sparkling new lighthouse rose above the beach. And, as their fame grew even wider, a luxurious wing was added onto the new white tower. In it, a newly-formed Lighthouse Society could celebrate its social functions.

The years fled by. Then one rainy night the Society was holding its annual formal dinner. The guests were dining by candlelight and dancing to a string quartet when suddenly: "Look, a red flare over the sea!"

The cruel rocks had trapped another victim. As the dinner continued, the rescue crew fought the storm in desperate relays. The shipwreck proved the most horrible of all. There had been an explosion aboard ship, mangling many of the survivors. They flooded the lighthouse, filling the ballroom with confusion and overturning tables. The dinner guests were stunned.

Many of those shipwrecked were naked and hysterical. Worst of all, some even had black or yellow skin.

The lighthouse's governing committee met in emergency session. The annual dinner — vital to their fund-raising efforts — had been ruined. There was ugly murmuring: "Something must be done."

And so separate buildings were constructed for shipwreck victims, in order that the new lighthouse would not be spoiled nor the social functions of the Society be disrupted. But soon other problems arose, and at last the chairman of the lighthouse called a general meeting: "Times have changed. The lighthouse has grown and taken over many new and important functions. The old work of lifesaving is now a hindrance to our tasks."

An angry debate followed and a minority protested: "But we are a rescue station!"

"If we stop saving lives, we have lost our reason for existence!"

Yet they were shouted down. When the ballot was taken, the lighthouse had discontinued its lifesaving operations.

An angry minority left in protest and moved to a rocky reef down the coast. In the midst of great hardship, they built a new lighthouse. Over the years, the fame of this new little lighthouse spread, until one day there arrived a delegation of benefactors: "Such a courageous crew deserves more than a dilapidated lighthouse. We have raised funds for an entirely new building...."

A modern lighthouse soon arose into the air, and professional crews began to battle the tides. Then, with the passing of time, lifesaving operations became less and less frequent.

Again, members divided into bitter factions. Angry arguments flared into the open, and a few left to build a third lighthouse. So it was with a fourth lighthouse, and a fifth, and a sixth....

Until today, there are many expensive and exclusive lighthouses along that stormy coast.

Many are the ships that wreck upon its cruel rocks, and many are the lives that are lost.

---

1. Phyllis Theroux, "Two Kinds of Jars," *Sign Magazine,* February, 1973.

2. Paul Reps, compiler, *Zen Flesh, Zen Bones* (Garden City: Doubleday).

3. Anthony de Mello, *The Song of the Bird* (Garden City: Image, 1984), p. 140.

4. Robert Fulghum, *Uh-Oh* (New York: Villard Books, 1994), pp. 153-157.

5. Daniel Juniper, *Along the Water's Edge* (New York: Paulist Press, 1982).

8

Faith Imagination And Preaching

Paul Scott Wilson in *Imagination of the Heart* wrote,"In the northern conifer forests of the United States and Canada there are a variety of birds in the grouse family which seek winter shelter under the snow. Often when I have unknowingly walked too close to one's hiding place, I have been startled as it thundered up through the surface and past the tops of the trees. I have turned only to see a fine sunlit dusting of snow falling in its flight path. Sometimes imagination is startling and wonderful like that. I have been told, however, that many grouse die when freezing rain traps them under a thick crust. The imagination of many of us who preach may similarly be trapped. We need a way to set it free."[1]

Using faith imagination is an ingredient of creative worship. Richard Lischer in *Theories of Preaching* wrote: "One of the most neglected dimensions of preaching, that of the imagination, is addressed by Joseph Sittler in his Beecher Lectures of 1959."[2] Sittler saw imagination as an evocation, a perception, fusing vision and speech, nature and grace. One of its functions is to fuse the theology, the what, and the rhetorical how of each text. He defines imagination as "the process by which there is reenacted in the reader the salvatory immediacy of the word of God as this word is witnessed to by the speaker."

Imagination is awareness, uncovering insights and understandings, seeing into by seeing beyond, and creating links and relationships between things. To recognize God's revelation in an Incarnation of grace in the natural world is one of the functions of the imagination of the Christian. Yet the imagination does not just function in a cognitive manner, but is a *power* that operates on the affective as well. Recognizing our need for God's grace (God's

109

presence and promise of deliverance), and accepting that grace, both dying with Christ in baptism *now* and rising with him *then*, we live with both grace and nature. We are dead to sin but not finally. Only the imagination can accept such paradox.

Active imagination can awaken the inner world, provide energy for new insights and new actions, and with love transform images into presences. There is spiritual reality as well as physical reality, a spiritual universe from which the visible world draws its chief significance. In the imagination we see from the "inside" where everything is possible. The true illusion is that imagination and reality are opposites.

The poet Marianne Moore once said that what we want is real toads in an imaginary garden, but I think what we really want is God's grace in a human Christ in a "locatable garden."

Carl Jung believed in the imagination. He told of an artist who had great difficulty in learning to use his imagination. He tried all sorts of things, but one day as he was waiting for his train, he noticed a colorful poster of a scene in the Alps on the wall. There was a snowcapped mountain in the distance, a waterfall at one side, and a green hill with cows grazing on it in the foreground. He tried to imagine himself into the picture and walked up the hill. The moment he went over the top of the hill he stepped into another dimension of reality by using his imagination. He discovered the same series of images each time, but the moment he doubted the value of what he was doing, the images disappeared.

Imagination suggests that we can die to the old consciousness, the old harmful habits, in order to enter a new existence. We can view our present problems as pain or opportunity. When the will is ill, we use our faith imaginations.

I have seen emotional healing through the imagination. I have experienced it, as well. Therefore to me it is a reality that images and attitudes can change, that by balancing the physical and the spiritual, we move toward wholeness. Our active faith imagination can free us from limitations upon the possible and help us let go of weak mooring posts to anchor ourselves in God.

I stared at the two articles. One I had read with interest and enthusiasm, savoring each word, sensing the scene, imaging the events. The author by her style of writing convinced and excited me. I was intrigued and pleased. The other article I plodded through, frequently getting stuck in the mire of reason, logic, and most of all, boredom. Over and over, because of the way the article had been written, I said aloud to myself, or to the author, "So what?" while what I really meant was "How dull!"

It was the contrast between the styles of the authors that made me stop and think. Both had written on the same subject, one academically and the other autobiographically, and it was then I recalled Yeats' words:

"God guard me from those thoughts men think
In the mind alone;
He that sings a lasting song
Thinks in a marrow-bone."

Words that touch the emotions, the marrow-bone, are lasting songs when we have been moved by their "music." We need not deny the need for rational, logical thought, for facts and information, but if that is all we hear, we finally cover our ears.

Reading our text as prose has value but reading it as poetry is experiencing the text with intuition and imagination. The twentieth century person until recently has been starved for the imaginative. Today we celebrate imagination in techniques such as "creative visualization," guided faith meditation, intensive journaling, dream work, and books that teach us the power of the creative imagination:

Creative visualization. The technique of using your imagination to create what you want in your life is called creative visualization. For our purposes, we can visualize being more open to God's spirit in our lives and in our sermons. There are two ways to visualize: letting go of thoughts and being receptive to the ideas, images, and impressions that arise, and consciously choosing and creating what we wish to see or imagine, being open to the surprises that arise.

Imagery is taking time to picture what one wants to do in the exact setting. It is "seeing" what might happen and anticipating various reactions both good and bad in order to do careful planning, problem-solving and decision making.

Those who use creative visualization affirm it as a means of dissolving the barriers we have created through negative thinking. "I can't do it. Nothing is coming to mind. I'll just borrow that old sermon of ..." What we tell ourselves in our mind is the foundation on which we form our perceptions of reality. Creative visualization affirms: "This, or something better, now is. Thanks be to God."

Guided faith meditation. We live in the gap between the conscious and the unconscious, whose bridge is the imagination. The human imagination is the proper place for the divine spirit to play. Faith imagination is inviting Jesus into that setting or situation, talking with and listening to what might be said, according to one's faith and God's surprises. In faith imagination we let go of expectations and remain open to the surprises of God.

Intensive journaling. Ira Progoff, author of *At a Journal Workshop, Intensive Journaling,* interested in the process of what feeds and brings to fruition creative acts in people, discovered techniques for activating the unconscious into consciousness. One of these he calls "dialoguing with your work."

Dialogue with the text and your "work" on the sermon. Enter the story and write six to eight "stepping stones" of how the text got to where it is. Then in a meditative stance personify the sermon (or text), feeling its presence and creating a relationship with it. Write what you wish to remember. When you have finished your dialogue, read what you have written and return to it throughout the week until you are ready to write the sermon. Dialogue with the finished sermon.

Clustering poetry. To write a clustering poem is a way of remembering, an act of the active imagination. At the center of the paper write one word you wish to explore with your imagination. It may be the theme of your sermon or a word from the text. Circle the word. Close your eyes and let images, thoughts, and feelings come and go, writing them around your central word. When you feel you are finished, open your eyes and write them into a poem.

Dream work. When imagination is creatively alive, people are rich with dreams. Unburdened by logic or disillusionment, they are free to see freshly, as if for the first time, for to dream is to be

112

human, to be free, to be creative. Dreams are the beginning of creation, and stories and sermons can grow out of dreaming, expressing in words the visions, dreams, and experiences that can be shared with others. Sermons and worship services shaped out of the imagination and shared in love give delight.

Whether one is compelled or called, if one is committed to the process of extending one's dream and translating that dream into artwork, something new emerges which carries both the creator and others into a depth dimension of experience, healing and making whole the artist and his or her audience.

The biblical writers understood dreams as a way that God spoke to men and women. To dream is to sleep, to let go of conscious thinking and will, and "drop down into" or "rise up to," metaphors for sensing a different reality from daytime awareness. The whole of reality cannot be contained or experienced in the waking hours alone. Today many modern psychoanalysts speak of dreams as a voice of inner truth. Dreams are the way we story our lives in sleep.

Carl Jung also told of a conversation with a chief of the Pueblo Indians who explained that they thought of dreams as "thoughts of the heart." Dr. Jung appreciated this metaphor and recognized that such "thoughts of the heart" push on us for our attention and if ignored, we then attempt to solve our problems and temptations in useless and destructive ways.

Dreams can help us uncover truth, face our temptations, as well as cure fears and fulfill desires. There are, however, many people who suspect or are embarrassed by believing in such "superstitions," as they call them. It is understandable to suspect what we do not know nor have experienced. Yet we know that everyone dreams, whether we remember dreaming or not.

Jung believed in the power of dreams to reveal, energize, hope and heal, for they are the imagination of the unconscious. An autistic child, emerging from withdrawal, was asked to define good parents, to which the child replied, "They hope for you." As does our faith imagination. Overwhelmed by adversity or anxiety, fantasizing, imaging future possibilities, and trust in God provide hope.

The imaginal process is seen in films as well. As long ago as 1939 *The Wizard of Oz* dealt with the imagination, beginning as a black and white documentary until the cyclone hit and everything spun around and around and into color, the "dream." The ego, the center of consciousness, that had been situated in Kansas, was now carried off into another realm, into a dream where rational "rules" did not apply, where the inanimate became animate. The teacher became a witch, which she is symbolically in many children's imaginations; the wizard, a bloated head, is whisked away by his own hot air; and the good witch, who has the power to restore relationships, reveals the energy within each of us to love and take care of our own lives. Thus, when we return to "Kansas," we are renewed by fantasy, by the story which reveals the power of the imagination to transform, heal, and renew. Sometimes the creative preacher preaches from films that are current and provocative on either the pros or the cons of the Christian life.

Books. Books written by creative authors energize the mind. In his *Imagining A Sermon,*[3] Thomas Troeger has written the entire book in the design of the process of writing an actual sermon. "An idea for a sermon flashes across your mind. You jot it down and start writing. For a moment the sermon flows. Then unforeseen difficulties become apparent, your creative energies fade, and you wonder whether the original idea was worthwhile in the first place.

"The pattern is familiar to most preachers. Imagination can be as capricious as the wind. After the initial gusts of inspiration blow themselves out, we face the hard labor of discovering the meaning of that revelation, which promised so much when it first seized our thoughts."

Frequently people with a desire, or a gift, to write or paint or pray, to bring something into being, discover creativity and imagination demand encountering solitude. The poet Ranier Maria Rilke, who experienced the loneliness of creative work, wrote *Letters to a Young Poet*[4] in which he advised, "Go into yourself and take whatever comes with great trust...."

Yet sometimes our talent or our desire feels too small, meager, minor even to try. It is then I remember the words Jean Rhys said to an interviewer in the *Paris Review,* which Madeleine L'Engle quoted in *Walking on Water: Reflections on Faith and Art*[5]: "All of writing (or whatever your task or talent) is a huge lake. There are great rivers that feed the lake, like Tolstoy and Dostoyevsky. And there are more trickles, like Jean Rhys. All that matters is feeding the lake. I don't matter. The lake matters. You must keep feeding the lake."

Sometimes we are unaware of the hidden gifts of our imagination and creativity. Because of our busyness we may lose or ignore time to reflect on the creative, artistic person that we were meant to be.

Through prayer and contemplation (being open to the energy, guidance, and power of the Holy Spirit), inner and outer attentiveness, incubation (input simmering within the unconscious), relaxation and playing with the images of the text, questioning assumptions, talking with others, exchanging ideas and information (with the author of the text, the persons in the text, the congregation who will hear the text), creative visualization, attention to dreams, journaling, reading, and watching creative films, our imaginations will be set free.

---

1. Paul Scott Wilson, *Imagination of the Heart* (Nashville: Abingdon, 1988) p. 11.

2. Richard Lischer, *Theories of Preaching* (Durham, NC: Labyrinth Press, 1987), p. 243.

3. Thomas H. Troeger, *Imagining a Sermon* (Nashville: Abingdon Press, 1990).

4. Ranier Maria Rilke, *Letters to a Young Poet* (New York: W.W. Norton & Co., 1934).

5. Madeleine L'Engle, *Walking on Water* (New York: Bantam Books, 1982).

9

Affirmations Of Faith

To affirm what we believe together down through the ages does not mean we will agree with every word spoken in the affirmation, but we affirm each other's rights to speak it aloud in this community of faith.

These affirmations may encourage you to write your own. The worship leader invites participants to "affirm" their faith before the statement of beliefs:

1. I believe that one day heaven and earth will be one,
Male and female, young and old, rich and poor,
Heart and mind, body and spirit,
All creatures of the Creative Spirit God.
Laughter and tears will be united,
Joy and sorrow,
Celebrating and grieving,
Play and work.
Worship will be dance and song,
Word and silence,
Sacrament and symbol,
United in God the Parent,
Jesus the Christ,
And the Holy Spirit in Whom all things are one.

2. Affirmation for justice:
We await the new heaven and new earth,
The place where justice will be at home
And we shall all be one,
And all broken bonds be healed,

All separations united,
All divisions forgiven.
Sister and Brother of every color, race, and creed shall eat
At the banquet of God
And join together in the song and dance of life,
For compassion will be wed to power,
And softness to strength,
The poor to the rich,
   the young to the old,
        the slave to the master,
All will care for the sick and lonely,
   the poor and weak.
Then strangers shall be friends,
And heaven and earth renewed in harmony with God.
Death shall be no more,
Mourning and crying and pain will vanish,
And the weapons of war will be transformed into objects of peace.

3. I believe that God is active on our faith journey and with Meister Eckhart affirm: "... Learn to look through every gift and every event to God and never be content with the thing itself. There is no stopping place in this life. No, nor was there ever one for any person, no matter how far along the way they've gone. This above all then, be ready at all times for the gifts of God, and always for new ones."[1]

4. I believe in God the Creator of heaven and earth and of all creatures, beasts of the field, birds of the air, fish in the seas, and in Jesus Christ who reconciled and is reconciling all creation, and in the Holy Spirit who teaches and empowers us to take care of that creation. I believe in the church of Jesus Christ where love for all of the creation of God is preached and practiced, and in the sacred story that gives us hope, in which "ugly ducklings" become swans and children the sons and daughters, princes and princesses, of the Almighty Creator and King. Amen.

5. "His delight is not in the strength of the horse ... but the Lord takes pleasure in those who fear him, in those who hope in his steadfast love" (Psalm 147:10-11).

Moses put his trust in the Lord,
The Egyptians in their horses.
Pharaoh's hope soon drowned in the sea
That swallowed all his forces.
Swifter than the leopards, more fierce,
The enemy did ensue them,
Whose hope was not
In the strength of the horse,
But the Lord whose love pursued them.
This I believe.

6. Mother Teresa once offered to build an orphanage with "three pennies and God." Of course they thought she was joking and told her so. "You cannot build an orphanage with three pennies!"

"With three pennies it may not be possible," she agreed, "but with three pennies and God, anything is possible."

I believe in God for whom all things are possible,

And in Jesus the Christ who said, "For God all things are possible," living out these words in his life and death and resurrection,

And in the Holy Spirit who enables us to experience the presence of these possibilities.

For I believe in the possibility of each creature to love and work with God,

And in community inside and outside of the church. Amen.

7. I believe in God who has given us the gift of life,
And in Jesus Christ, who came to show us abundant life,
And in the Holy Spirit who opens us to receive this gift
And share it with others.
I believe in the kingdom of God that is here and now
And is yet to come, for I believe that we are witnesses to the resurrection,
And of the living Lord,
Made in the image of God,
Called to do justice,
Love mercy,
And walk humbly with our God.

I believe that sin is putting ourselves
At the center of the universe,
Yet until we love ourselves,
We cannot love another,
So I believe God first loves us
And in our acceptance of that love,
We love ourselves.
And I believe that the world is full of mystery,
Meaning, and mercy,
For I believe we are never alone
Because God is always in search of us,
Persuading us with yearning love.
I believe that life is good,
That dying is part of the gift of life,
Returning that gift to God
Who graces us with new life
In Christ our Lord. Amen.

8. I believe in God the Creator and in the gift of our senses; in smell and sight, in taste and touch, and in new life in spring and in us.
I smell the perfumed rose in spring,
I hear the birds returning, sing,
I feel the gentle sun and rain,
And see the golden fields of grain.
I taste the berries ripened red,
And melons from our garden bed,
When skies above are blue and clear,
And all outdoors shouts, "God is here!"
Amen!

9. I believe in God who created a love that is being stored up as an inheritance, and I trust that in this love there is strength and blessing.
  I believe that for one human being to love another may be the most difficult of all our tasks and the work for which all other work is but preparation, for love ripens slowly, changing as it grows.

I believe that to be able to give love without thought of reward is to love God and neighbor as oneself, an expression of maturity and trust in God, for it is in human love relations that we discover something of the love of God, although we cannot equate this love with the love of God.

And I believe Christ has redeemed and renewed us in God's love so that we may dare to love, to ripen, to become worldly for oneself for another's sake.

And I believe in the Holy Spirit whose witness is love, whose gift I do not accept except through God. Amen.

10. I believe in God the Creator and Giver of beauty,
And in Jesus Christ, God's Word of beauty,
And in the beauty of words, such as Paul's, "Finally, whatever is true, whatever is honorable, whatever is just, whatever is pure, whatever is lovely, whatever is gracious, if there is any excellence, if there is anything worthy of praise, think about these things" (Philippians 4).

And I believe in the Holy Spirit who enables us to do acts of beauty through genuine unselfishness, affection, and kindness, in the remembrance of God's love and beauty.

11. When the children of Israel sang their song of triumph after crossing the Reed Sea, the angels in heaven joined them in singing. God asked the angels, "Why are you singing?"

They replied, "We are singing because your children, the children of Israel, have been saved today."

Then God rebuked them by saying, "Do you not know that the Egyptians who drowned today are also my children?"

I affirm the love of God and the oneness of all God's creation.

12. The psychiatrist Carl Jung once quoted one of his patients as saying, "If only I knew that life had some meaning and purpose, then there would be no silly story about my nerves."
I believe Easter is the wind whispering,
The birds singing,
The spring flowers blooming,

The church proclaiming, "There is meaning.
There is new life.
There is resurrection in the name of Christ,
Our Savior. Alleluia!"

13. I believe "For everything there is a season ..." (Ecclesiastes 3:1-8):
A time to create
And a time to repeat,
A time to celebrate
And a time to wait,
A time to accept
And a time to reject,
A time for touching
And a time to be apart,
A time for pizza, ice cream and cheesecake
And a time for broccoli, bananas, and black beans,
A time for lilies and daisies and daffodils
And a time for barren trees, sleet and snow, and sleeping seeds,
A time for creativity and newborn words and images
And a time for tradition, rooted symbols and sacraments,
A time to worship ... always a time to worship,
For this is the meaning and purpose of time.

14. I believe there is meaning in all things, far beyond our understanding or appreciation, that there are two ways of seeing, one on the basis of sense perception, the other from "above," "in Christ," where all things become new.

I believe all reality has infinite, transcendent significance, waiting to be discovered through God's grace and the gift of the Holy Spirit, leading us into the wonder and awe of its eternity.

I believe that the seen stands for the unseen, that God is both hidden and revealed, known and unknown, and that the imagination is the bridge between the body and the spirit.

And I believe Christ is the Son of God and by believing, I believe we have life in his name!

I believe that we are conquerors of all things through Jesus Christ who loves us, and nothing will separate us from the love of God.

This I believe. Lord, transform my unbelief! Amen.

15. I believe in God the Creator and affirm and pray:
I thank You God for most this amazing
day: for the leaping greenly spirits of trees
and a blue true dream of sky; and for everything
which is natural which is infinite which is yes
(I who have died am alive again today,
and this is the sun's birthday: this is the birth
day of life and of love and wings: and of the gay
great happening illimitably earth)
how should tasting touching hearing seeing
breathing and — lifted from the no
of all nothing — human merely being
doubt unimaginable You?
(now the ears of my ears awake and
now the eyes of my eyes are opened)[2]

16. The Lord is my healer,
I shall not hurt.
He makes a peaceful place for me to rest.
He leads me into deep waters that restore my soul.
He guides me in the way of light.
Even though I walk through the Valley of Loneliness,
I will feel no loss,
For You are with me.
Your people and Your presence comfort me.
You give me work and meaning and wholeness,
And I am filled with Your love.
Surely peace and hope will be with me all the days of my life,
For I will live with You forever. Amen.

17. "For all that has been — Thanks!
To all that shall be — Yes!"[3]

123

18. Blessed are the trees that stand
Planted by the streams,
Their branches never wither,
Or so it seems.
Dressed in the lovely colors of the leaves
And fruits they wear,
The blossoms of the apple
And the golden pear.
Blessed is the one who walks
Upright in God's sight.
They shall prosper as the tree
In God's strength and might. (Based on Psalm 1)

19. I believe in God who created song to fill the universe

And in Jesus, who with his friends, sang as they left their last meal together

And in the Holy Spirit who fills our hearts and voices with song and opens our mouths to sing.

I believe music is the way we praise the One who created creatures "in our image," from the morning stars who sang together to the children who shout for joy.

I believe in the possibility of music to re-create the world with hope. And I believe in a singing world in the sanctuary and in the street, in the sky and in the sea.

20. I believe in God, whose word brought the world into being, and I believe in Jesus Christ, who died a parabler for God to rise the Parable of God, and I believe in the Holy Spirit, who puts sacred stories into our ears and mind and heart, moving us to faith and hope and love. And I believe in the church, the people of God's story, called to tell God's story to the world. Amen.

21. I believe in God the Creator, Maker-Giver-Owner of heaven and earth.

And in Jesus Christ, "fairest of all creatures, ruler of all nature."

And in the Holy Spirit of the living God in beast and bird, sea and tree, and all creatures in the web of life.

And I believe in the Scripture's story that gives us our sense of identity and meaning and mission.

And I believe in those who hear The Word and respond to it. Amen.

22. I believe in a universe not made in jest but in justice by a Power mysterious, holy, and present,

And in the glory of the Word to warn and warm, made flesh to dwell among us, Jesus the Christ.

I believe in the solitude of the individual whose kingdom of heaven is within and in the solidarity of all people whose vision is of freedom, liberation, and well-being for all of creation.

I believe in women and their power of relationship, imagination, and intuition,

And in men and their ability to reason and reflect,

And in the Holy Spirit of God who integrates us into the wholeness of woman-man, who is neither male nor female. Amen.

23. I believe that God reveals through the Word, creates through words, and calls us to enflesh and embody God's words.

I believe that God speaks in dreams and in the imagination.

And in silence. Not the silence inflicted upon marginized persons, but the silence that is the peace of God which the world can neither give nor take away. Amen.

24. I believe in the resurrection and the life now and forevermore through Jesus the Christ, who has broken down the dividing wall that is the hostility between us and others and us and God.

I believe that by grace we have been saved through faith, the gift of God.

And through the Holy Spirit we are built together spiritually into a dwelling place for God (Ephesians 2:22).

25. I believe in God, Creator and Judge of all, and in God's power, and I believe in Jesus Christ who died and was raised to show us the secret of God's power, and I believe in the Holy Spirit who is God's power among us and between us, helping us in our weakness. Amen.

26. I believe in hope because I have already received what I hope for: trust and peace with God.

I believe in the God of hope, because it is God who has given me trust and peace within.

I believe in Jesus Christ who died on the cross so that we may be united in hope and peace with God.

And I believe in the Holy Spirit who has flooded our hearts with that hope and love of God.

27. I believe in God and in God's "righteousness," God's desire and ability to be a faithful Covental Parent.

I believe in Jesus Christ as Lord, the name by whom we are saved and set free.

And I believe in the Holy Spirit, the power that comes from God to make us one in trust and obedience.

28. I believe God is my treasure,
And where the treasure is, there is the heart.
And I believe in Jesus Christ, the treasure trove,
And in the Holy Spirit who reveals and unlocks that treasure.

29. I believe in God who calls us into trust,
And in Jesus the Christ whose trust in God blessed his life with true believing,
And in the Holy Spirit who comforts us when others' actions are deceiving.

And I believe in the power of God to teach those we love how to treat us, for no one but God can fill our incompleteness.

30. I affirm and thank God for foolish people who see visions and preach promises we can neither see nor touch.

I affirm and thank God for unbelievable life that births buds and blossoms in the spring and sprigs of hope in new words and new life and new wineskins.

I affirm and thank God for words that never pass away, for silly sons and daughters who sing God's story into history. Amen.

31. I affirm life and love and God,
and stories that affirm suffering and pain ...
... doubt and despair ...
... joy and beauty ...
... singing and praise ...
... benedictions and blessings.

32. I believe in God, the loving Parent, who created all persons in the image of God.

And I believe in Jesus Christ, the child of God, made in the image of God.

I believe in the Holy Spirit, the Spirit of God that enables us to know who we are and what we are to do.

I believe in the church as the body and spirit of the Triune God.

And in that power to create and love, because we are made in God's image.

33. I believe in Love as its own reward, for I believe that despair does not alter the reality of things nor destroy the joy of the dance of life.

Because I believe in God who is Love,

And in Jesus Christ who knew that Love and taught and showed us how to live that love,

And in the Holy Spirit who empowers us to love without being sure of the answering love of the other.

---

1. Meister Eckhart, *A Modern Translation* (New York: Harper & Row, 1941).

2. e e cummings, *Complete Poems* 1913-1962, Vol. 2, p. 663.

3. Dag Hammarskjold, *Markings* (New York: Ballantine, 1964), p. 74.

10

Prayer In The Act Of Worship

In the morning, while it was still very dark, he got up and went out to a deserted place, and there he prayed.

The act of worship is dialogue between God and God's people. It is a way of corporate praying, praying in public, for prayer is an integral part, the essential aspect, of our relationship with God. Prayer is the bridge of our relationship with God, the source of our strength and hope and healing.

Some persons reviled Jesus one day as he was walking through their part of the town. But he answered by repeating prayers in their name. Someone said to him, "You prayed for these men, did you not feel incensed against them?" Jesus replied, "I could spend only of what I had in my purse."

No one can live without spiritual resources. Prayer is the water in the well that allows us to survive. Jesus said to the Samaritan woman that he was "living water" and prayer not only provides us with strength to survive, but to thrive. There is spiritual bankruptcy without praying.

We learn to do by doing. In worship we join together in the practice of prayer, in learning how to pray by listening to a leader of prayer, and by praying oneself. As the disciples asked Jesus, "Teach us to pray," so we ask the "messenger" of God, the one who brings us God's word and will, to lead us, teach us, in prayer.

We learn through liturgy. William H. Willimon tells the story[1] of one of his parishioners being harassed at work by an unscrupulous supervisor who did everything possible to humiliate him and make his life miserable. The parishioner was afraid that one day his supervisor would push him too far and he would "bash his brains out."

Together they talked about his feelings and the pastor suggested that he might pray each morning before going to work, asking God to help him endure this man's attacks.

"I never thought about prayer," he said.

"Oh, yes. Jesus urges us to bless our enemies and to pray for those who persecute us," replied the pastor.

"I never heard us pray for enemies on Sunday morning," he said.

What do we learn about prayer on Sunday morning?

There are five kinds of prayer: confession, praise, thanksgiving, intercession, and petition. In public worship we praise and thank God. We confess, intercede and petition for the individual, the community, the nation, and the world.

Through Sunday prayer we are reminded of our calling — to glorify and trust God — and of God's grace in our lives.

Jesus prayed in public as well as in private. He went to the synagogue to pray, and to the mountain.

In private prayer we tell God everything as honestly as we are able, inviting God into our brokenness and asking God to heal and guide and show us what to pray for and what to do.

Public prayer, however, is not private prayer. Public prayer is the leading of the people of God in their prayers as a community of faith, as a people of God. Therefore, one's own fears, doubts, concerns, even celebrations, are inappropriate at this time and place, for the leader of worship must always face the danger of getting in the way of worship. Worship is not a public performance. It is a prayerful participation.

The leader of worship makes choices between "free" or "liturgical" prayer, between "spontaneous" and "written" prayer in their leading.

As Protestants we have a rich heritage of prayer. The use of written prayers encourages fuller participation on the part of the congregation. Willimon reminds us, "Ordered, carefully worded, historic prayers give objectivity and stability to the service, catholicity, scriptural soundness, historical awareness, and continuity with the prayers of the church at all times and places."[2]

Both free and liturgical prayer have strengths and weaknesses. In free prayer we are open to the Spirit, to particularity and concreteness and warmth, and to the danger of a rambling "sermonette," especially if the preacher is not preaching the sermon at that service of worship. It would be well to ask ourselves whether we are informing or lecturing God or listening to God.

Spontaneous and liturgical praying are two ways of encountering and being with God, and both ways require planning. In teaching we say, "She who fails to plan, plans to fail." With careful planning, we are then free to be open to the Spirit's movement. One way of planning might be:

1. Meditate on the scripture, sermon, season of the church year, and serious concerns of the congregation.

2. Write a simple outline.

3. Complete the prayer.

4. Pray for guidance before praying for the congregation.

5. Pray publicly without the written prayer.

Honor silence. For many, silence is painful and the thought of linking prayer with silence is a new one to many Christians. We are used to verbal praying in the church, but this is not the only way of praying.

Praying with silence is becoming still in the presence of God, still enough to listen and hear our own deepest needs, to share them honestly with God, and to be aware of the thoughts and images that arise in that context.

Exercises in silence bring a surprising sense of satisfaction and surprising images of dreams, myths, sacred stories, fantasies, visions, and voices as well. As we relax in silence in God's presence, a light in the darkness is kindled, and new awareness comes into the consciousness. Studies indicate that rather than mystics being out of touch with reality, not another factor has been found to correlate as highly with psychological balance as does mystical experience.

There is a need for silence after the invitation to the prayer for confession, for each of us has individual as well as corporate concerns. This is also true for intercession, petition, and thanksgiving as well. We might say, "Let us offer to God those persons for whom we would now intercede ..." and "Let us come before God with our individual thanks for specific acts of God's grace in our lives ..." and "In these moments we pray our particular prayers of petition...."

Many pastors suggest a topic for prayer and invite parishioners to pray in silence, using their own thoughts and words. Paper at the door of the sanctuary or in the pew encourages people to make prayer requests for public praying in the pastoral prayer.

Honor language. Language shapes our thoughts and actions. As a woman I use inclusive language because:

1. Language shapes the way we think and act. The silence about women, by women, and toward women excludes women. Much of the language in the church excludes me. There is an awareness today of the need for language to include all people, especially in the church because the church should embody Christ's message of love which excludes no one.

2. We worship One God who is father-mother of us all. Worship as praise of God requires inclusive language to be "whole," for the object of that worship, God, is whole. God imaged as male lacks the reality of Oneness. God, the Source of all life, cannot be only "part" and is beyond all imaging in human forms. As the pun states, "The world is made up of Eves as much as atoms."

3. Theology and worship that is only seen and expressed through male eyes can lack the feminine traits of intuition, imagination, "heart." Without generalizing, for many men are warm, passionately compassionate persons, there has been a tendency in the past in worship on a predominance of words, noise, to the exclusion of silence.

The other side of silence is that of the "unspoken" voices of women and other marginized persons, the "null" worship, what is not said or sung, for hymns reflect and teach theology.

So much of theology has been defined from a male point of view, such as "sin" defined as "pride," "self-love" and "will to power." (I attended seminary the first time at Union when Niebuhr reigned and it was a good reign. I was, however, unaware at that time how excluded I really was.)

Such a male definition of sin is not how women experience sin, which to many women (or should I say me?) is separation, doubt, and unfaithfulness.

To exclude is to make "outside." In Mark's gospel Jesus goes over "to the other side" over and over again as a symbolic act of "binding up" separateness, acting as a "bridge" between the insider and outsider, the Jew and the Gentile.

The God I worship loves and heals and "includes." Including is loving and healing in itself.

All teaching and worship is shaped by social, political, and cultural conditioning. We do well, therefore, to ask how our approach to worship is formed by our language, by what we say and do not say. Thus, I both appreciate and affirm silence for listening and negate silence by refusing to be silent in the language of worship.

Made in God's image, we create "images" of God. Nelle Morton calls God "the Great Ear" who listens to the heart and sound of the universe.[3]

For me worship is "bonding," bonding all persons together with God, the insider and the outsider (both sides of the "sea"), in the act of the worship of God.

Bonding is sharing "bread" in the Eucharist and in the world, for the act of worship feeds us for our work in the world.

The dual task of listening and being silent in worship, as in living, which is what worship is for me, living intentionally in the presence of God, helps us become aware and hopefully more loving, compassionate people through the grace of God ... *all* of us!

Prayer is an essential act of worship, for through prayer we can become aware of what is beyond sensory perception and connect with that reality. In prayer we know how deeply we are loved by God, giving us freedom from what blocks us from living fully: fear, fanaticism, doubt, despair, selfishness, and separation from others, for freedom from fear is the freedom to love.

1. William H. Willimon, *Preaching and Leading Worship* (Philadelphia: Westminster).

2. *Ibid.*

3. Appreciation to Maria Harris for her "speaking" in *Teaching & Religious Imagination* (San Francisco: Harper & Row, 1987).

11

Prayers

The following prayers were written to help us pray and create our own prayers for the service of worship:

1. Saint Francis' Prayer:
Lord, make us the instrument of Thy peace
Where there is hatred, let us sow love
Where there is injury, pardon
Where there is doubt, faith
Where there is despair, hope
Where there is darkness, light
Where there is sadness, joy
May we seek not so much to be consoled as to console
Not so much to be understood as to understand
Not so much to be loved as to love.
For it is in giving that we receive
It is in pardoning that we are pardoned
It is in dying that we awake to eternal life.

2. A Prayer For Daily Praying:
May my quest be ever unfolding
    My restlessness unceasing
        My path unending
            My love increasing.

3. Opening Prayer: *(In unison)*
Lord, hungry for hope
    in a time when heaven and earth
    are shaking within us and about us,

Help us endure
    with trust and patience
    to the end.
When we seek a sign
    of your presence among us,
Remind us
    through your Word
    of your words
    that will not pass away.
Birth again
    within our hearts the promise
    of the power that is present
    in your promise
    of your presence
    even unto the end of the world. Amen.

4. Dear God, halfway through the day it opened ...
The cactus by our backdoor.
I should have grabbed my camera or my brush.
Its beauty was too much. It could not stay.
Halfway through the evening it had gone.
One cannot capture beauty any more than time,
I know now the meaning is in its moment.
Keep me awake and alert, O Lord. Amen.

5. Without faith prayers are simply words.
I name you ...
Be butterfly and behemoth,
be galaxy and grasshopper, star and sparrow ...
Be caterpillar and comet, be porcupine and planet,
sea sand and solar system, sing with us,
dance with us, rejoice with us,
for the glory of creation, sea gulls and seraphim,
angle worms and angel host, chrysanthemum and cherubim
Be![1]

6. Dear God, we gather in your name. Some of us are weary and need to rest in your presence. Some of us have been tested beyond our human strength and need your energy and power. Some of us are full of joy in the glory of your creation. Help us all to be simple and poor enough to see you in all things so that we may trust all will be well, knowing all things are possible for you. In Christ's name we pray. Amen.

7. Dear Lord, we have come to this holy place in this holy hour, blessed by the Spirit of Christ, to pray, to listen, and to see, for what we see is what we get. Amen.

8. Dear Lord, I hear your call and follow your way, though the night be dark and the day be dreary, and though I doubt and stumble and fall, I hear your call. I will always be too weak to be your prophet. Give me your wisdom. Amen.

9. Lord, help us keep alive a holy wonder, an amazing astonishment, a sense of the mysterious.

10. Leader: Thank you for the gift of the Holy Spirit that gives power to the imagination to see "visions" and "dream dreams," to heal hopelessness and create possibility. Show us a way out and be with us on our way. Open our eyes to the rainbows of hope and the promise of reconciliation and rebirth. In your mercy ...
People: Hear our prayer, O Lord.
Leader: Grant us the living faith that finds the extraordinary in the ordinary. In your mercy ...
People: Hear our prayer, O Lord.

11. Praise God the living Spirit for the dancing energy of every molecule, cascading mountains and bubbling children's laughter, Shostakovich's symphonies, and autumn's riot of color. Amen.

12`. God, open our ears and eyes to the particular places where love happens here and now among us, symbols of your incredible love, so that we may see and experience the invisible in the visible.

We say "God is love" because we have seen Your love in the story of Jesus of Nazareth, a particular man in a particular place at a particular time. Open us to the wonder of the ordinary become extraordinary, Love putting on human flesh. Amen.

13. God, You are our Pied Piper in the world, gently persuading us into a relationship of love and wonder through symbols and stories and songs, helping us move forward out of the past's bondage into the future's possibilities. Help us to feed and celebrate the life of the imagination, the key to a living faith. Amen.

14. The mystics of the Hasidic tradition wrote: "Do not think that the words of prayer as you say them go up to God. It is not the words themselves that ascend; rather it is the burning desire of your heart that rises like smoke to heaven. If your prayer consists only of words and letters, but does not contain your heart's desire, how can it rise up to God?"

15. Lord of Creation, open my heart and mind and eyes to each butterfly and bird and bush, all beauty, all creation as filled with Your divine presence. Thank You for the persistence of Your love that is like a lover who will not take "no" for an answer. Amen.

16. God, bless our cries and tears, the language of the infant and the compassionate, the friends of Lazarus and the widow of Nain.

Let our tears become sacraments of praise and psalms of petition to You who collect the tears of the innocent and the cries of the guiltless.

Hear them as soundless expressions of our deepest feelings of longing and sadness, of expectation and joy.

Let our beatitudes of tears rise up to You as sacred songs on wings of hope, formed in and flown from the heart,

Spontaneously watering the soil of our spirit so it may be kept moist and fertile for growing,

And transform these human streams of humility into fuel that flames our acts of passion for the poor, the bondaged, and the abused

In the name of Jesus, who wept. Amen.

17. Dear God, Father-Creator of the world,
Son, dearest freshness deep down,
Holy Ghost with warm breast and bright wings:
Hear our prayer of
Praise for Your grandeur,
Thanksgiving for Your greatness,
Confession for having trod, not reckoning your rod,
Of intercession for those seared with trade, smeared with toil,
Of petition for morning and bright wings. Amen and Amen.

18. Gracious God, as a mother feeds her young, protects the helpless ones, broods over their suffering, lifts them with hope and
faith and bright wings, I pray Your Spirit lifts me into the light of
Your grandeur that I may know Your love and sing Your praise,
world without end. Amen.

19. My son began and half-finished, brought it home to me.
In its roughness I saw its meaning ...
How like my life: plans half-finished, words unsaid, dreams un-
done,
Yet the attempt ... it was begun,
And though incomplete, it holds my books,
Doing what it was meant to do. Lord, help me do so, too. Amen.

20. Dear God, create in me a fresh heart, new eyes and ears, open
hands, and fearless feet. Dig out my ears so I may hear Your call to
love and serve, fill me with energy and enthusiasm, patience and
perseverance, and awaken me to the precious people on my path,
that each day I take time to celebrate Your wonder and will for me.
Amen.

21. "Thou that hast given so much to me,
Give one thing more — a grateful heart;
Not thankful when it pleases me,
As if thy blessings had spare days,
But such a heart whose pulse may be
Thy praise." (George Herbert)

22. God of Abram and Sarah,
We are amazed that you still have gifts for us.
Like Sarah and Abram we assumed that your work was finished,
that from here on out we were on our own.
But you, O God, are full of surprising gifts.
Our world is not barren,
but it is pregnant with new possibilities
for justice and freedom, for homes and land and health.
And so with Sarah we laugh, laugh in amazement at your
promises, laugh at the despair that you are shattering. Laugh,
standing at the threshold of a new day, we laugh. Amen.

(David Greenhaw, Lancaster, Pa.)

23. Lord, You are our shepherd, our keeper, our provider, protector, and physician. We shall not want. You give us green pastures and still waters to restore our spirit, and when the waters are rough, You lead us even through the valley of the shadow of death. You are with us through evil, and comfort us with Your rod and staff, preparing a table before us, where our cup overflows. Goodness and mercy follow us as we dwell with you forever. Now hear our thanks and praise and our petition that such fullness may come to all people and all creatures, for You are our Creator and risen Lord. Amen.

24. Dear God, how frequently we cry to You for comfort, asking that You restore unto us the courage to create, to love, and to live abundantly. We thank You for the comfort of Your love which we find in Your Word, in Your world of nature, and in Your people. We pray that we may be and give that comfort to others, in Christ's name. Amen.

25. Dear God,
I cannot wrap a mountain up
Or give the Sea away,
I cannot make the Robin sing
Or buy a sunny Day.
I cannot cause a Flower to bloom

Or catch the Wind at play.
I cannot paint a Sunset,
But I can pause and pray.
Thank You, Lord, for the majesty
And mystery of Your creation
Within and without. Amen.

26. Lord, we confess that You have created us for wonder. We do not control creation, but cooperate with it in "abiding astonishment." We have, however, neglected to feed our spirits with wonder and the simple things of life we take for granted. Sprinkle our spirits with the dew of Your delight so that we may again see all of life in the attitude of gratitude. So we pray with Paul: We are afflicted in every way, but not crushed. We are perplexed, but not driven to despair. We are persecuted, but not forsaken. Struck down, but not destroyed.

27. Pray the old prayer of our Lord with new meaning:

Our Father: Parent of young and old, rich and poor, in sickness and in health. Who is in heaven: Parent who is Somewhere and Spirit who is everywhere. Hallowed be Thy name: Majestic is God's name.

Your kingdom come: Let Your reign come now among the just and the unjust and in the time to come. Your will be done: The hungry fed, the naked clothed, the prisoner visited. On earth as it is in heaven: We are one in God. Give us this day our daily bread: And help us share it with others. And forgive us our trespasses (debts, wrongs, sins):

Our complacency, our unconcern.

Overcome our separation from you,
As we forgive those who trespass against us.

As we overcome our separation from each other.
Lead us not into temptation: Keep us mindful of who we are.
But deliver us from evil: In time of trial, deliver us from despair,
The bombs we make and store,
The land we pollute and cover with concrete.
YOURS IS THE KINGDOM AND THE POWER AND THE GLORY. AMEN!

141

28. *Our Father,* Living Father-Mother of the poor and rich, the weak and strong, the sick and well, the young and old.

Who is in heaven, And out there ahead of us.

Hallowed be your name, the Most Holy One.

Your kingdom come, The time is now.

Your will be done, for Your ways are not our ways.

On earth as it is in heaven, and around our needy world.

Give us this day our daily bread, And help us share it with others. Feed the hungry, clothe the naked, visit the lonely, speak hope to the helpless.

And forgive us our trespasses, Our complacency, our selfish actions.

As we forgive those who trespass against us, Keep us mindful of who we are.

And lead us not into temptation, Help us let go of ego and selfish needs.

But deliver us from evil, The bombs we support, the land we pollute, the hungry we ignore.

For thine is the kingdom And the power And the glory. Amen!

29. David prayed, "God, You are my God, and I long for You. My whole being desires You; my soul is thirsty for You, like a dry, worn-out, and waterless land. Let me see You in the sanctuary..."

Let me *hear* You, God, in the pulpit that speaks Your words in images we can enter.

Let me *touch* You, God, in the baptismal font, for my soul is thirsty for You.

Let me *taste* You, God, in the bread and wine of the holy feast in which You are always present.

Let me *see* You, God, in the windows of the sanctuary through which we view Your glorious creation.

Come to me in the cross, the picture of Your love.

30. David prayed, "Let me see how mighty and glorious You are. Your constant love is better than life itself." And David concluded, "And so I praise You. I will give thanks as long as I live." David the singer, David the psalmist, perhaps the writer of the beloved Twenty-third Psalm, named the God he worshiped " my shepherd."

31. Day by day.
Oh, dear Lord,
three things I pray —
To see Thee more clearly,
Love Thee more dearly,
Follow Thee more nearly,
Day by day.
  —Richard of Chichester, ca. 1197-1253

32. The poet T. S. Eliot wrote: "Of all that was done in the past,
you eat the fruit, either rotten or ripe.
And the Church must be forever building, and always decaying,
and always being restored.
The Church must be forever building, for it is forever decaying
within and attacked from without;
For this is the law of life; and you must remember that while there
is time of prosperity
The people will neglect the Temple, and in time of adversity they
will decry it.
What life have you if you have not life together?
There is no life that is not in community,
And no community not lived in praise of God.
Even the anchorite who meditates alone,
For whom the days and nights repeat the praise of God,
Prays for the Church, the Body of Christ incarnate."[2]

33. Lord of every creature wild and tame,
Who gave them life, and food, and name,
Lord of the sunlight, Lord of the sea,
Lord of the heavens, the beast, the bee,
Lord of all life, of plant and tree,
Thank You, O Lord, for loving me!

34. Almighty God, fill our hearts with love for You and our neighbors,
fill our minds with gratitude for new life,
fill our bodies with the joy of Jesus' resurrection,

so that we may praise You with singing
and share with others the good news of Your love. Amen.

35. Most gracious Maker, the Giver of life and hope, we thank You for our creation and for the gift of hope. Help us discover in our love for You and for our neighbor as ourself, the way to express and share that hope with others. Amen.

36. God, the loving Parent, waits for our return. As children of God, let us pray our Prayer of Praise: Thank You, God, for those who led us by the hand when we were young, taught our minds and hearts to be open to Your word and will, fed our imaginations so that today we may welcome, lead, teach, and feed children everywhere, as well as the "child" that is within each of us. Amen.

37. Saint Francis' Creation Prayer: Praised be my Lord God with all His creatures; and specially our brother the sun, who brings us the day, and who brings us the light; fair is he, and shining with a very great splendor. Praised be my Lord for our sister the moon, and for the stars which He has set clear and lovely in heaven. Praised be my Lord for our brother the wind, and for air and cloud, calms and all weather, by the which Thou upholdest in life all creatures. Praised be my Lord for our sister water, who is very serviceable unto us, and humble, and precious, and clean. Praised be my Lord for our brother fire, through whom Thou givest us light in the darkness; and he is bright and pleasant, and very mighty, and strong. Praised be my Lord for our mother the earth, the which doth sustain us and keep us, and bringeth forth divers fruits, and flowers of many colors, and grass. Praise ye, and bless ye the Lord, and give thanks unto Him and serve Him with great humility.

(Ask participants to illustrate the prayer. As you pray together ask illustrators to show their verse with the appropriate words. Display the illustrated prayer on the church hall walls. Use watercolors, colored felt pens, paint, chalk, fingerpaint, and/or crayons.)

38. Jesus Christ, fill my emptiness with your presence, my mind with your direction, my heart with your grace. I thank you for your presence meeting mine in love. Amen.

39. Pass the Peace: Stretch out your hand now and pass the peace in the name of the Prince of peace.

40. A Prayer for the New Year:
When the song of the angels is still
And the candles of Advent are out,
When wild winter returns with its chill
And faith is frozen in doubt,
Then let the message of Christmas begin again ...
    Peace to all nations
    Good news to the poor,
    Power to the weak,
    Food for the hungry,
    Sight for the blind,
    Hope for the meek,
    Fire for the altar of love within.
    And may your New Year be blessed with God's presence and love. Amen.

41. Three Fathers used to go and visit blessed Anthony every year and two of them used to discuss their thoughts and the salvation of their souls with him, but the third always remained silent and did not ask him anything. After a long time, Abba Anthony said to him, "You often come here to see me, but you never ask me anything," and the other replied, "It is enough to see you, Father."
    It is enough to be with with You, God.
    Let us pray in silence in the presence of God.

42. Dear God, Source of life and love, as we feel your "yes" in our lives, help us to respond with our "yes" to You and our neighbors, in Christ's name. Amen.

43. Take our ordinary, common, material gifts and transform them into our loving responses to Your love, In Christ's name.

44. Most gracious God, we face the paradox of being responsible and yet trusting You, the paradox of interpreting a story that was written in a different time and place and pretending we know what the story means. Make us new people through Your promise and mystery, people who know and do not know, but with Your help and grace, in both the wisdom and the ignorance, attempt to love. Amen.

45. God, Creator of the Universe that came into being through your word, "Let there be," help us to hear and enflesh your words of correction and challenge and comfort, given to us through the parables of Jesus, the Word. In his name we pray. Amen.

46. To the Creative Spirit who creates all things, whom we call God; To the Loving Son who reconciles all things, whom we call Christ; To the Great Spirit who directs and relates all things, whom we call Holy Spirit, hear our prayers of confession, intercession, praise, thanksgiving, and petition:

Blessed are You, holy one of Being,
the One expressing through each of us,
as our God, Ruler beyond time and space,
who holds us in life,
who supports the unfolding of our integrity,
who brings each of us to this moment for blessing.
Blessed is Your name. Amen.

Guided Faith Imagination Praying:

47. Paul said that the church is the body of Christ and we should respect one another because of our differences, because we are one in Christ (1 Corinthians 12:12, 14-21, 26).

Meditate on this image by closing your eyes, placing your feet on the floor, hands in lap, and body erect but comfortable. Breathe deeply and imagine yourself as a member of the church with your gifts and responsibilities. Become aware of the whole "body" and the sense of community in sharing gifts. See your role in that body. Become aware of a particular person in your community of faith and experience Christ's love flow between you. Feel the flow of joy ... of sorrow ... of pain. Do this with as many people as you like as long as it feels right. Then become aware of your gift and see if there is anything you would like to do because of the persons you have just seen in your imagination, or anything you would like to change. Experience an acceptance of yourself and your gift as a part of the whole body, and as a body experience the joy of all its parts and express your appreciation in some way. When you are finished, return to this place and open your eyes.

48. I invite you now to do with me a guided faith meditation by closing your eyes, placing your feet on the floor, hands in lap, and breathing in and out. You are walking in God's creation when you see a burning bush. You come closer to the bush to see what is happening and hear a voice call your name. Listen now to what the voice says to you about creation and saving the environment. *(Pause)* You reply. *(Pause)* Then, knowing you can return to the Voice in your imagination whenever you wish, come back to this place and open your eyes.

49. Matthew 27:45-46: Jesus cried from the cross in his time of trouble, "My God, my God, why have you forsaken me?" "Eli, Eli, lema sabachthani?" In times of crises, we too cry out, "God, where are you now?" Center yourself by filling yourself with silence. Breathe deeply. Slowly allow the crises or decision you are now facing to emerge. Tell God honestly how you are feeling and accept whatever words, images, or feelings come to you. Rest with them for a while and then invite Jesus into your imagination, asking him to comfort, correct, or advise you. *(Pause)* Do not be anxious or impatient. Return to this meditation, for resolution may take several hours or several days.[3]

50. Peter and the beloved disciple run to the tomb and you follow them. When the beloved disciple reaches the tomb, he looks inside. "The grave cloths are still there," he says. Peter enters the tomb and sees the grave cloths in one place and the face cloth in another, and the beloved disciple enters, looks, and believes. Then Peter and the beloved disciple return home. You are alone. Jesus is dead. His body is gone. You stand outside the tomb and cry. When you finally look inside, there are two angels dressed in white, one sitting at the head and the other at the feet where the body of Jesus had been. They ask, "Why are you crying?" "They took the Lord and I do not know where they put him." A new voice speaks. "Why are you crying? For whom are you looking?" It must be the gardener. "If you have taken him away, tell me where you have put him." He calls you by name! Listen to Jesus call you by your name now. Turn and speak to him, telling him what is on your heart. As you approach him, he says, "Do not touch me, but go and tell my friends that I am going to my Father and your Father, my God and your God." You sit in the silence alone, in amazement, too shocked to move. Jesus is alive! Jesus is not dead! You jump up and run to tell the others, "I have seen the Lord! This is what he said!" When you are ready, return to this place, knowing you can be with Jesus whenever you want, and open your eyes.

51. Read John 14:1-2. Do a "good-bye" guided imagery: Close your eyes and place your feet on the floor. Become quiet and take three deep breaths. Become aware of walking in a park, a meadow, or a garden. Feel the warm sunshine. See the growing grass, the colorful flowers, and the blooming trees. As you walk up the path that slopes up the hill, you come to a dwelling with a sign over the doorway: "In God's House There Are Many Dwelling Places." When you are ready, go inside and choose the room you will go within, noticing how you feel as you enter. You become aware that this is the dwelling of the person to whom you are saying good-bye. Interact with this person as long as you like. Ask the person for a symbol or gift or word you may keep to remember him or her and say good-bye in any way that feels comfortable for you. Then go to the front door and say good-bye to the whole house, remembering the people and the gifts you have shared there. Walk out to the meadow and look at the gift you have brought. Feel the warmth of the sun and the beauty of the surroundings and take note of your thoughts and feelings. When you are ready, return to this place and open your eyes.

52. Be comfortable in your chair with your feet flat on the floor, hands in lap, and eyes closed. Take three deep, slow breaths. Imagine yourself walking in a meadow. Observe the colors and scents of the flowers. Feel the warm sun soothing your back and arms. Walk slowly. *(Pause)* You experience great joy with a sense that this is the way life was meant to be ... except for your dream. If you only had your treasure, you would be completely content. Feel the obstacles to obtaining that for which you are searching, ways you get stuck. You plan steps to obtain it and ask for any help you need. *(Pause)* Suddenly you notice something on your path. It is that for which you are searching. You stoop down and look at it and are surprised that it is here, that it is possible for you to have it. Feel that joy now. *(Pause)* What must you do to obtain it? Describe how you feel to God and tell God what you will do with your treasure. *(Pause)* Now you must decide whether you will bury it and return later to purchase the meadow and the treasure, leave it there for someone else to find, or take it back with you now. You are aware that it will call for sacrifice, hard work, on your part. You may even have to give up all that you now have to possess it. Ask Jesus to help you make your decision. *(Pause)* When you decide what to do, finish for now, and when you are ready return to this room.

Feedback: Did you find your "pearl"? Were you surprised by what you found? How did you feel when you found it? Why did you or didn't you sell all you had in order to buy the "pearl"? What must you let go in order to obtain the pearl? Is this possible and if not, what can you substitute for the pearl? Do you have an image for your treasure? If you are willing to share what your treasure is, tell us about it now.

53. Recall the place where you were most at peace, most filled with joy. Return to that place in your imagination. Do a symbolic fantasy. Imagine yourself sitting on top of a mountain, on the seashore, or in a forest of trees. Decide what is the most comfortable place for you before proceeding. Then sit there with an imaginary companion or alone and feel God's peace and joy. Invite Jesus to sit with you. Talk with Jesus about whatever is on your heart or in your mind at this time. Observe the place. What is it that offers you hope here? Fill yourself with the feelings of this hope or joy so that you can return to the city or wherever you live filled with that hope. Choose a symbol to take back with you that will remind you of this place, of God in this place, such as the memory of a peaceful, flowing brook, a star in a black velvet sky, the face of a loved one. Take your time choosing a symbol (such as a leaf, a seashell, a flower).

54. In the last story of John's gospel Jesus came to his friends in the dark, in the early morning, on the shore. I invite you to close your eyes and in the darkness use your imagination to be on the shore now. It is dark. It is early morning. You feel the wet sea mist sweep over your face. You hear the sea gulls crying and smell fish frying. You look in that direction and see Jesus, who calls you to come and eat with him. You run to Jesus, for you know your need for bread and fish. In the darkness Jesus whispers, "Do you love me ... more than these?" With food in your mouth, you shake your head and mumble, "Yes, Lord, you know that I love you." "Feed my lambs." Jesus asks the question again, this time in a loud, firm voice. "Do you love me ... more than possessions or success?" "Yes, Lord, you know that I love you." "Take care of my sheep!" Then Jesus stands up and shouts, "Do you love me ... more than your own life?" Answer him in your own words, remembering the many times you have denied him, as Peter did. *(Long pause)* "Feed my sheep!" And when you are ready, return to this place and open your eyes.

55. Write and pray an "ACTS" prayer: Adoration, Confession, Thanksgiving, and Supplication, such as the following based on John 19:

ADORATION: As I enter more deeply into the passion story in this encounter with Pilate and the trial of Jesus, I am having a lover's quarrel with you, for if I am to do as Pilate says, "Look at the man!" God, I am reminded of evil and injustice and the suffering of the world.

I could adore You that You have allowed creatures free will, but at Creation the scale seemed to be tipped. Look at the man! Look at the world! Lord, may I return to adore You after I have confessed? For now let me simply adore and praise Your persuasive love.

CONFESSION: When I look at the man, Lord, I can only confess that I am part of the crowd. I look at the man and hear his words, "For this I was born ..."

I confess I do not always trust Your love and will. I doubt Your mercy, for when I look at the world, I want a miracle of justice. I want proof of Your presence in such a world as this ...

THANKSGIVING: And Jesus answered Pilate, "My kingship is not of this world ..."

I thank You, God, that with free will, with choice, You have given me the gift of faith to believe what I cannot see nor touch, to believe in the possibility of Your love and its persuasive power.

I thank You for the truth that is more than propositions, sectarian doctrines, or creeds, for the truth that is revealed in the Person of Christ, the Parable of You and Your love.

I thank You for this story that was written so that we might know that Jesus is the Christ, the Son of God, and that by believing have life in his name.

SUPPLICATION: So, Lord, I ask for forgiveness and for a firmer faith, that the echo of Your love might even pervade the world, as we look at the man sacrificed for all people.

Whenever I must play Pilate and decide what to do with Jesus, help me refuse to bow before Caesar and hand him over to be crucified.

I pray for vision to look at the man and see there Your persuasive love so that I may have the voice to witness to that love. In Christ's name now I pray. Amen.

56. John 18:1-12

ADORATION: You call to the storm and the waves cease, the thunder stops, and the lightning disappears ,and You calm the storms in my life as well.

You turn the common, ordinary, everyday water into extraordinary wine and my common, ordinary, everyday experiences into extraordinary messages from You.

You heal the eyes of those who were born blind and those of us who cannot see and reveal to me the meaning of Your presence.

Is it so surprising then that 600 men with weapons and war experience fall to the ground before Your word?

I too take off my shoes in Your presence, for this is holy ground.

Yesterday I recalled how Charles, when he was seven, and saw the sun come up over the ocean, ran to his room to "get dressed for the sun," and I dressed in my best for Communion in chapel for the ... Son.

CONFESSION: I confess with Judas that I betray You in the times I do not speak Your name or Your message. Have I lost confidence in the message of the "good news" or in me? Forgive me. As the preacher from England said in chapel yesterday, "It is jolly hard."

Forgive my lack of courage in my convictions, my lack of engagement in Your story, and my lack of encounter with Your world.

Forgive my doubt and lack of trust. Forgive my despair over my disappointments and lack of patience, knowing You have a better plan for me, for You want the best for me. Forgive my emptiness and lack of vision, my blindness and lack of action.

Forgive what I have done in selfishness, and out of my own need and disappointment and unawareness, and forgive what I have not done out of my fear and heaviness and wounded memories.

THANKSGIVING: Thank You for revealing who You are, for helping me become aware of who You are and of the meaning of Your name and Your presence in my life.

Thank You for Your authority. I too fall to the ground, and for giving me a sense of that authority I have in Your name, as Your child.

Thank You for revealing the amazing secrets of love and nature and the unconscious, as I seek to know You and Your will in my life, to know the purpose and meaning of the greatest of all Your gracious gifts, life itself.

Thank You for drinking the "cup" which the Father gave You for our sake.

SUPPLICATION: Because of these prayers of adoration, confession, and thanksgiving, I ask now for further and future awareness, deeper understanding and greater trust in Your promises and in Your presence.

I ask for courage and boldness to believe and to speak in my own voice Your will for the world, the message of peace and love and justice and healing

I ask for increased imagination, the gift of play and celebration, and the ability to hear and heal in Your name, so that I may, through You, know my fear and my desire, to drink the "cup" which the Father gives me. Amen.

57. John 18:13-27

ADORATION: Dear God, Creator of story and world through the word, I adore You and Your Word and Your story.

Through the Word and the words You reveal the meaning of discipleship, and of Jesus' authority and relationship through words. I stumble, heavy with my humble words, and You comfort me with words as a mother comforts her children.

I make mistakes and think selfish thoughts and You correct me with words as a loving Father.

I am complacent about the evils in the world, about the needs of the hungry and homeless, the abused and the oppressed, the ignored and the marginalized, and You challenge me with words of living spirit.

O Lord, Father-Mother-Spirit, Your name is above all names and Your Word is above all words. Hear the words of my mouth as I give You praise and adoration.

CONFESSION: I confess how often I wait outside Your door afraid to go in, afraid You may recognize me and call me by name, afraid You will remember the things I should have done and did not do and the things I did do that were displeasing in your sight.

I confess my denial of discipleship. It is easier for me to be with people with whom I agree than with those who think and speak differently. It is easier for me to stay home than to go out. It is easier for me to write about suffering in South Africa and El Salvador, the ghetto and the graveyard, than to encounter and engage the homeless and hungry, the lonely and hopeless. It is easier for me to be in prayer than to be in service, and easier to nurse my wounds than to be a wounded healer. It is easier for me to tell my story thank to listen to the other's story. Lord, forgive me.

THANKSGIVING: I thank You, God, for becoming a human.

I thank You for helping me to become a human and all the good that that implies.

I thank You for stretching me, pushing me, pulling me into places I do not want to be, because You know better.

I thank You for Jesus' teachings, for the disciples, the ancient storytellers, and the writers who wrote "all these things so that we might know Jesus is the Christ, the Son of the living God."

I thank You for preachers and teachers, scholars and parents, for those who push the broom and those who push our minds and hearts to know when knowing is to love.

I thank You for love, for showing love and being love and providing love in all the many varieties of ways.

SUPPLICATION: Therefore I pray — let me love the teacher, let me be the teacher;

give me friends who will "get me in," who will bring me to Jesus when I am paralyzed, who will love me when I am unlovely;

give me the courage to preach in public and not only in secret places, and to learn from the authority of Jesus.

And, oh, Lord, give me a voice, let me find my own voice, so I will not stutter nor deny when I am asked who Christ is and who I am.

Let me be a worthy disciple in the courtyard, in the courtroom, or wherever You call me to be compassionate. In Christ's name. Amen.

---

1. Adapted, Madeleine L'Engle, *A Wind In the Door* (New York: Farrar, Straus & Giroux, 1973), pp. 203-204.

2. T. S. Eliot, *Collected Poems 1909-1962* (New York: Harcourt, Brace & World, 1964).

3. Elaine M. Ward, *Faith Imagination and The Spirit* (Prescott, AZ: Educational Ministries, 1997), p. 37.

12

Benedictions

Worship closes with the benediction, an invocation of divine blessing, a symbol of completion and empowerment: "Go now into the world in the name of God ... Jesus the Christ ... and the Holy Spirit ... taking your worship of God into the world."

Benedictions are the last words the worshiping congregation hears; words that not only bless but remind the people, commission the people, that what they have heard and seen and done during the hour of worship enables them to "report for duty" in the name of God, to be God's representatives in the world outside the walls of the sanctuary.

Carol Doran and Thomas Troeger tell the story of a pastor who wanted to encourage his congregation to attend the adult education program after the worship service. In his enthusiasm and commitment to education, he withheld the benediction until the closing of that program. There was universal revolt. Without the benediction the people felt they had no closure. They could not leave their pews without completing the worship service. More important, they did not feel the sense of empowerment for ministry that is conveyed by the benediction.[1]

While many feel the worship service is only the beginning and is not complete without our work in the world, the living out of our response to God's love and grace, others want and need the sense of order and structure of the familiar form and shape of their traditional worship service.

1. The disciples were full of questions about God.

The master said, "God is the Unknown and the Unknowable. Every statement about God, every answer to your questions, is a distortion of the truth."

155

The disciples were bewildered. "Then why do you speak about God at all?"

The master said, "Why does the bird sing?"[2]

Go now in the name of God who created the Song and the Singer, and Jesus Christ who is the Song we sing, and the Holy Spirit, who fills our hearts and voices with song, enabling us to sing. Amen.

2. "Be like the bird, who
Halting in his flight
On limb too slight
Feels it give way beneath him,
Yet sings,
Knowing he has wings."[3]

Go into the world with your song in the name of God who gives us "wings" and Jesus who teaches us to sing, and the Holy Spirit who enables us to "fly" with faith. Amen.

3. There was a woman who wore a sword in her breast, but because she did not want to burden others, she covered it with her cloak. One day she met another woman, groaning and moaning and groping in the dark with her hands. "What is the matter?" she asked. The woman explained that she was blind and in need of a staff. The woman who could see looked all around but she could find no staff, and at last she took the only thing she had and gave it to the woman. It was the sword in her heart. The blind woman thanked her and, using the sword, said, "This is a good staff." For the first time the woman saw the purpose of the sword in her heart.

Go now into the world in the name of God who knows "the swords in our hearts," and Jesus who changes swords into staves, and the Holy Spirit who enables us to see and be healed so that we may heal. Amen.

4. All of his life the monk had prayed for a visitation by Mother Mary. At the last moment the Mother arrived. The monk was in ecstasy. But in the midst of this mighty moment, the bell rang to feed the hungry. "Oh, Mother, I must leave. I am so sorry. Please stay." He offered Christ's food to the poor and returned to his cell, miserable with disappointment. To his surprise, however, Mary was still there. "You stayed!" he exclaimed. "Yes," she replied. "However, if you had stayed, I would have gone."[4]

Go now into the world in the presence of God to offer Christ's food to the hungry, by the power of the Holy Spirit. Amen.

5. The student complained to his rabbi, "David wrote the psalms, but what can I do?" The rabbi replied, "Tell them."

Go now into the world and tell God's story of the good news of Jesus Christ, through the gift of the Spirit. Amen.

6. Long ago and yesterday when stories roamed the earth, teaching and listening, an emperor heard of a wise sage. His reputation for wisdom and erudition preceded him and brought him to the attention and the throne of the emperor. "I have heard much about you, for they say you are a wise and learned man. They say you have powers of transformation, that you can read and heal people's minds. I too am a man of learning and would like you to prove to me your powers. In my hands behind my back is a bird. Is it alive or is it dead?" The sage was silent. The sage could not speak for he was afraid that as the result of what he said, he could kill the bird if the bird were still alive. So he did not speak. The emperor looked at the sage and smiled and the sage looked into the eyes of the emperor and was silent. The emperor waited. The silence hung heavy as a sword over the head of the sage and then he said, "Your majesty, the answer is in your hands."

Go now in the name of Our Loving Lord with the answer in your hands. Amen.

7. "May the God of hope fill you with all joy and peace in believing, so that you may abound in hope by the power of the Holy Spirit" (Romans 15:13).

8. My words fall from my lips as stones
I stub my toes upon,
While God with gentle whispering
Communicates the dawn

157

And rising, sings the world awake
In chorus with the bird.
I celebrate God's ability,
Creating through the Word.

Go now in song and in the name of God who creates singing and the world, and Jesus Christ who teaches us how to sing, and the Holy Spirit who enables us to hear the music of all creation. Amen.

9. A moment of silence for prayer.

Go now in the name of God who speaks in sheer silence, and Jesus Christ who taught us to pray silently, and the Holy Spirit who enables us to hear and to speak inside and outside of silence. Amen.

10. "Let those love now, who never lov'd before:
Let those who always lov'd, now love the more."[5]

Go now in the name of God, which is Love, and Jesus who showed us the meaning of Love, and the Holy Spirit, who enables us to love. Amen.

11. In worship we are bonded and bound in love;
the powerful and the poor,
the insider and the out,
the soft and the hard,
the dove and the hawk,
the strong and the weak,
the bondaged and the bonder,
for in worship we believe that all will be well
and all will be one, for
    this is our promise
     this is our plea
    this is our prayer

Go now, from this worship, into the world, so that you may story your words to inspire your hearers, to feed their spiritual hunger, and to enable them to feed and serve in Christ's name with you now and in the time to come, that we may all be one. Amen!

12. Once the eagle, crane, all birds were proud and free,
Soaring high above the earth, over the sea.
Now the air is filled with smog instead of birds,
"O beautiful for spacious skies ..." forgotten words.
Seas are poisoned by our waste, earth by our mess.
Someday earth and sea may be no more ...
Unless ...

Now in the name of God who made the world, and in his son,
Christ Jesus, who came into the world to save the world, and in the
Holy Spirit who empowers and enlightens the world, go out into
that world and be a light and power in Christ's name. Amen.

13. God, bless all seagulls flying free,
Each butterfly, each bird, each bee,
Each dove and pigeon with your care,
Hear hungry, hurt, and high-honked geese
And bring them safely home,
All weary travelers of the air,
So they may rest in peace.

Go now in the name of God who gives us peace and love,
through our Lord Jesus Christ through whom we have obtained
access to this grace of God's love that has been poured into our
hearts through the Holy Spirit. Amen.

14. Trust grows slowly, like a tree,
Strong and sturdy, steadily,
Stretching leaves and limbs above,
As arms that hold us in their love.
Everyone needs trust to grow,
Deep roots of faith so they may know
And show ... trust.

Go now in the name of God who gives life and hope, and Jesus
the Christ who shows us how to live and trust and hope, and the
Holy Spirit who provides imagination, friendship, and wishing.
Amen.

15. I whisper "Thou"
The rest is silence
More would be what I do not know
More would be what I do not need
More would be redundant, for You
   already know all my ... more.
Go now in the name of God for whom all things are possible, and in Jesus Christ who calls us to come and follow him, and the Holy Spirit who enables us to trust, follow, and love, in Christ's name. Amen.

16. Go now in the name of God who yearns for our wholeness, and Jesus Christ who is the Health of the world, and the Holy Spirit who enables us to be healed and to heal. Amen.

17. Go now in the name of our gracious God, and Jesus Christ who shows us God's grace, and the Holy Spirit who enables us to become graceful people. Amen.

18. Go now into the world in the name of God who proves his love for us, and in Jesus Christ through whom we have received grace and reconciliation, and the Holy Spirit who pours God's love into our hearts. Amen.

19. Now, in the name of God who gives life to the dead and calls into existence the things that do not exist, and Jesus Christ, our Lord who was raised from the dead, and the Holy Spirit who gives us hope, go into the world with the promise of God.

20. Go now into the world with the peace of God which the world can neither give nor take away, in the name of God who shows no partiality, and God's son with whom we are joint heirs, and the Holy Spirit dwelling within us. Amen.

21. Go now in the name of God who parents children, and Jesus Christ, who showed us how to love children, and the Holy Spirit, who unites us in one family, in Christ's name. Amen.

22. Go now in the name of God who created water, and Jesus Christ is who is the living water, and the Holy Spirit who enables us to drink. Amen.

23. Go now into the world telling the story of God who loves us, of Christ who redeems us, and the Spirit who gives us energy and life. In Christ's name. Amen.

24. Go now in the name of God who created the wind and the waves and holds us in steadfast love, and in Jesus Christ who commands the wind and the waves with authority and love, and in the Holy Spirit who enables us to trust in God's abiding, steadfast love.

25. Now may God, who is for all of time and everywhere, be with you in your feelings, in your thoughts, and in your actions. In Christ, our Lord, empowered by the Spirit. Amen.

26. Go now in the name of God, who has created the Sea and the Story, and Jesus, who leads us to the Sea as the Parable of God, and the Holy Spirit, who enables us to trust and to jump, bringing our stories into being. Amen.

27. Go now in the name of God who loves justice and mercy, and in Jesus his son, who showed us how to live and forgive, and the Holy Spirit who enables us to work for peace and reconciliation among all creation. Amen.

28. When Picasso was 85 years old, he wandered among a retrospective of his paintings in Cannes, France. Hundreds of his works, from the first he did as a young man to the latest of the master, hung on the walls of the gallery. A woman stopped him and said, "I don't understand. The beginning pictures are so mature, serious and solemn, and the later ones, so different, so irrepressible. It almost seems as though the dates should be reversed. How do you explain it?" "Easily," Picasso replied, eyes sparkling. "It takes a long time to become young."

Go now into the world, little children of our living Lord, in the name of God the Parent, who hugs the world in Christ, and the Holy Spirit who guides us in and out of childhood. Amen.

Advent Benedictions

29. The candles shine through the darkened church.
Tonight is Christmas Eve.
God bless each person here with peace,
May love and joy and hope increase,
Before the people leave.

Go now into the dark, bringing your light of love and joy and peace in the name of God, our Giver, Jesus Christ, who shows us what it means to give, and the Holy Spirit who enables us to bless in Christ's name. Amen.

30. Go now singing this night the song the angels sang —
Peace and good will — and run with the shepherds to his manger
bed to see God's Word.
May you bring your gifts and kneel with the wisemen three,
And may God's love fill your hearts and homes from this night on
So we will live more carefully, aware of one another
And of Him. Amen.

31. Christmas is over
'Til next Christmas day,
Candles and cards are all put away,
Bright decorations have been taken down,
Stored in the attics all over our town.
But we will remember though Christmas is gone,
Love for each other goes on and on and on ...
Go now in the love of God. Amen.

Lenten Benedictions

32. Now may beauty and the spirit of Christ live in your heart, for what is real is seen by the spirit and touched with the heart. Christ is risen!
Congregation: He is risen indeed!
All: Amen!

33. Moon had a message for man and woman and called Insect to come and carry the message to earth. The message of Moon was, "As I die and in dying, live, so you in dying will live also."

Insect took the message of Moon to earth and on the way met Hare. "Where are you going?" asked Hare.

"I have a message from Moon to man and woman. Moon said, " 'As I die and in dying, live again, so you in dying will live also.' "

"Insect, you are so slow. Let me take it," said Hare, and Insect gave the message to Hare.

Hare ran off fast and in his hurry, when he found man and woman, said, "Moon has sent you a message that in dying, Moon dies, so you too in dying shall perish."

When Moon heard what Hare had said, Moon was angry and took a stick and hit Hare on the nose. And that is why hares have split noses and men and women think that when they die, they perish.

Go now into the world, knowing that what we live by we die by. What we think we live by. Christ *is* risen! Amen!

34. Waken, lilies Easter-white,
Rise, you purple clover,
Dogwoods blossomed in the night,
Wintertime is over.
Roses, throw your thorns away,
Death forever sever.
In the victory of Christ,
We will live forever.

Now go in the name of our gracious, almighty God who raised Christ from the dead, and in Christ who died and was raised by the glory of the Father, and the Holy Spirit who empowers us with freedom from sin in our baptism in Christ Jesus. Amen.

35. The report reached Nimrod's ears that Abraham was mocking the idols, so he ordered that the boy be brought before him. Nimrod turned his gaze on him and said imperiously, "Here is fire; worship it!"

"My Lord," answered Abraham fearlessly, "wouldn't it be better to worship water since it can put out the fire?"

"Let it be as you say: worship water!"

"Shall I do an injustice to the clouds which give the earth all its water?" Abraham asked.

"Very well then: worship the clouds!"

"But how can the clouds compare with the winds who have the power to scatter them?" the boy asked again.

"Then worship the wind!"

"The wind? What will He who directs the fire, water, clouds, and wind say to that? O you blind man! Don't you perceive the mighty Hand that guides the world?"

The king was abashed and, turning away, left young Abraham in peace.[6]

Go now into the world, worshiping the mighty Hand that guides the fire, water, clouds, and wind in the name of the Triune God.

---

1. Carol Doran & Thomas H. Troeger, *Trouble At the Table: Gathering the Tribes for Worship* (Nashville: Abingdon, 1992), p. 130.

2. Anthony de Mello, *The Song of the Bird* (Garden City: Image, 1984), p. 3.

3. Victor Hugo, "Be Like the Bird" from *A Child's Book of Poems* (Grosset, 1969).

4. Elaine M. Ward, *Bread for the Banquet* (New York: United Church Press, 1990), p. 117.

5. James Carroll, *Prayer From Where You Are* (New York: Pflaum Publ., 1970).

6. Nathan Ausubel, *A Treasury of Jewish Folklore* (New York: Crown, 1940).

13

The Sacrament Of Baptism

Baptism water is more than just water,
Baptism water is stronger than steel,
Baptism water lasts longer than longer,
Mixed with its blessing are words that will heal.
Baptism water is truer than really,
Baptism water is more than you see,
Love and acceptance and God-given, freely,
Promising you and promising me,
"Now you are a part of God's family."

Baptism is a "sacrament." "Sacrament" comes from the Latin word *sacramentum*, which in ancient times, such as the Roman Empire, was a standard, a long pole with an image of an eagle at the top and sometimes a banner with the letters SPQR (The Senate and People of Rome) as a symbol for the presence of the emperor.

There are two sacraments in the Protestant Church: Baptism and Holy Communion, which represent Christ's presence with us. Both use the physical elements of daily living — water and bread and wine. Without these "ordinary" things we could not live. In a sacrament the "ordinary" things become extraordinary, for with the word of God, they become God's presence in a symbolic way.

That "word" becomes part of the redemptive act of God through Jesus Christ. It is God's promise of God's grace here and now partially in the present but fully in the "time to come."

Baptism is a sign-act of the death and resurrection of our Lord which we remember and celebrate in worship. That event was experienced in our sacred story on the day of Pentecost (Acts 2:38) when Peter said, "Repent and be baptized, every one of you, in the name of Jesus Christ for the forgiveness of your sins. And you will receive the gift of the Holy Spirit."

Paul identified baptism with the death and resurrection of Jesus (Romans 6:4). As a pattern of spirituality, a gift of the action of God's grace, accepting us "as we are," it is well to remember baptism as an initiation into acceptance of the responsibility for this gift.

In baptism we are "born again" "with water and the Spirit" (Matthew 16:16; John 3:5) to be bold in the Spirit, to "die" to doubt and live anew with trust in God.

Baptism was an initiation rite of the early church to take the place of circumcision (Genesis 17:11), the sign of entrance into the covenant community, the church, the royal priesthood of all believers.

When baptism represents "salvation" it is based on 1 Peter 3:20-22, which refers to Noah and the ark, the "pledge of a good conscience toward God."

In most mainline Protestant churches baptism happens during infancy, and "confirmation" when individuals have a "conscience" and the ability to make a "pledge" for themselves.

With Jacob, the Israelites, and Jesus, in baptism we receive a new identity. When a baby is born, a bracelet with the baby's family name is placed on its wrist in order to identify the baby. We know to whose family the baby belongs. When a person is baptized, water is placed on the person in order to give that person a new identity. We know to whom this person belongs. We are God's children so that at baptism we are given a boldness to be whom we were meant to be, to become God's children by "adoption." "I can't do it. I am afraid" becomes "I can do all things in Christ," for "I" becomes "we" at baptism.

Baptism means we have joined a very large family that extends around the world. Having been loved, we respond with love out of gratitude, and even that is God's grace, for God is Creator and Lord of all, who loves us with unconditional love.

The infant was stripped naked, taken into the arms of the church's representative, and placed in a large tub of warm water. The child played joyfully in the welcoming water, as some of it

166

was gently poured over the infant's head. Dripping with sacramental water, the parents dried and dressed their child in baptismal clothes. It was a metaphor to be remembered.

Being dressed in new clothes reminds me of another metaphor of baptism: C.S. Lewis tells the story of Eustace, a spoiled and selfish boy turned into a dragon by sleeping on a dragon's hoard with greedy, dragonish thoughts in his heart. It was the outward semblance of his inner spiritual condition. His friends did what they could for him and were very sorry about his plight, and the dragon in turn helped them. Actually being a dragon transformed Eustace, and the pleasure of being liked and liking others kept him from despair. Then one night Eustace saw a lion, and the lion came right up to Eustace the dragon. The lion told the dragon to follow him to a garden where there was a well in the middle of the garden. Here the lion told the dragon to undress and bathe in the well. As the dragon scratched himself, the scales and skin peeled off as a banana peeling, but each time a new skin appeared over and over until finally the lion said, "You will have to let me undress you." Eustace was afraid of the lion's claws but he was desperate and so lay down. The first tear was so deep it hurt miserably and so did the removal of the skin, but at last he was again smooth and soft. The swim in the well transformed Eustace into a boy again and the lion took him and dressed him. It was Aslan, the redeemer of Narnia, the great Lion, the son of the Emperor over Sea![1]

John, on the island of Patmos, had a vision, a revelation. On the Lord's Day, being in the Spirit, he heard a loud voice like a trumpet. John wrote, "I turned around to see the voice that was speaking to me. And when I turned I saw seven golden lampstands, and among the lampstands was someone 'like a son of man,' dressed in a robe reaching down to his feet and with a golden sash around his chest" (1:12-13).

Some clothing is symbolic. The "long robe" is the priestly garment taken from Exodus (28:4, 27), while the "golden sash" is the royal emblem of the king (1 Maccabees 10:89). The custom of wearing new clothes on Easter, for instance, is not to display our appearance, but a symbol that represents putting on "new clothes," Jesus casting off his old body for the new.

Baptism is a gift of God, not of understanding, nor of the amount of water used. There may be a variety of ways to baptize, but what matters is God's presence and promise in the act.

Baptism is the first step in learning to see God at work in the world, to hear God's call to minister in and to the world, and to imagine life in a new and certain way. Therefore, we celebrate in a Rededication Service, recalling one's own experiences of baptism and its stories:

1. Each of us has our story of baptism. An old Cree was aggressively visited by the missionaries who invited him to church and wanted him to be baptized. The old man, however, did not want to go to church where he felt they "locked up" God within, nor did he want to offend the priest, so he said and did nothing. The priest became more and more persistent, reminding the old man that his wife and children came to church. "You should be baptized," the priest insisted. Finally there was nothing for the old man to do but explain to the priest. "I have been baptized. One day I saw the storm coming and the rain began to fall and the thunderclouds called. I went outside and took off all my clothes except for my breech cloth and stood in the rain. I stood and stood and I was baptized."[2]

Oh, for a baptism like that when every rain reminds us of who we are!

2. Without labeling them as such, there are powerful stories of baptism, of water healing as well as destroying, e.g., the story of Noah and the lesser known story of Naaman the Syrian leper.

3. Michael L. Lindvall tells two stories of baptism in his "A Child Is Born."[3] He tells of Angus McDonnell, who informed the pastor that his son, Larry, and wife Sherry, who lived in Spokane, Washington, would be visiting for the Thanksgiving weekend and because this was going to be a big reunion, they wanted him to "do the baby," as Angus put it, the next Sunday.

The minister explained to Angus that it was best for a child to be baptized in the church where he would be raised and the importance of the parents' commitment to the faith, for they would be asked to make some deep promises in the sacrament.

Angus was an elder of the church and the last of the patriarchs. He shook the minister's hand, thanked him, and proceeded to poll the members of the board, who voted 9 to 0 in favor of the baptism.

That Sunday little Angus was "done," and when the pastor asked, "Who stands with this child?" Sherry and Larry's large family stood, but not the extended family of the congregation.

After church the pastor noticed Mildred Cory, who always sat in the very last pew, sitting in the front row. She explained that her daughter, Tina, had just had a baby and thought it should be baptized.

The minister suggested that Tina and her husband call to discuss it, and Mildred faltered, "Tina's got no husband; she's just eighteen, and she was confirmed in this church four years ago. Then she started to see this boy who was out of school ..." and the story tumbled out.

The board asked questions when it came before them, especially whether or not they could be certain that Tina would stick to her commitment.

"Tina and little Jimmy are right here in this town where we can look after them and give them support." He did not have to say, "And not in Spokane."

The board approved the baptism and it was scheduled for the last Sunday in Advent, and on that day the church was full, as it always is the Sunday before Christmas. Tina came down the aisle, nervously, shaking slightly, holding month-old Jimmy. She was so young, so alone, and yet, the pastor could not help but remember another baby boy born so long ago into difficult circumstances, a boy whose mother had also been unwed.

The service was read and the question asked, "Who stands with this child?" He nodded at Mildred slightly to coax her to her feet and she rose slowly. Returning his eyes to the book, he became aware of movement in the pews.

Angus McDonnell stood up, and then a couple of other elders. Then the sixth-grade Sunday School teacher, and a new couple in church, and soon, before incredulous eyes, the whole church stood up with little Jimmy.

169

Tina was crying. Mildred held on to the pew. The scripture reading recalled: "See what love the father has, that we should be called children of God. God's love is perfected in us, for there is no fear in love, but perfect love casts out fear."

In that baptism, those words came alive; they were clothed with God's love and everybody felt it.

4. John D. Stoneking,[4] called frantically to the hospital, debated his theology of baptism while driving. Baptism is God's reception of new life as a gift of grace, which the receiver, young or old, has done nothing to deserve.

The baby was dead, labor was induced to force delivery, but the baby had not been born yet. The minister asked the question and felt the terror of what the mother must be feeling, knowing that the life she had nurtured for nine months was lying dead within her. Before saying "good-bye," those parents had to say "hello."

The baby was delivered at last and laid in the mother's arms, the only moment she would ever spend with her child, and the baby was given a name, as the minister spoke of God's love for this baby, no matter what had happened.

The pastor recalled that in the midst of tears, which is an authentic baptism by water and the Spirit, the baby was offered up to God and asked that Nathan Andrew be held gently and tenderly. Then four days later, parents, family, and friends, gathered for the burial of Nathan Andrew, for whom God grieved, as they did.

Shortly after they said hello, Nathan Andrew's parents said good-bye, knowing his life would never be forgotten, but held gently at the breast of God for all eternity.

5. Walter Wangerin, Jr., tells the story, "Baby Hannah,"[5] of Pastor Cheri and baptism at worship in a picnic shelter, the table covered with a bedsheet, the warm, sacred baptismal water in a glass salad bowl. Wangerin witnesses the sacrament and Pastor's Cheri's hesitation, "Hannah, I ..." Over and over she begins and stops, her only words, "Hannah, I ..." He cannot see her, surrounded by Hannah's thirteen godparents, but he can hear her words, "Hannah, I ..." At last he realizes why. Pastor Cheri, pastor and mother of Hannah, is crying. He pictures Hannah's birth as it had been described to him by Cheri. Of course, Cheri cries. Born in blood, and now the water of baptism. Pastor Cheri was the voice — of God and the love of God!

Wangerin then uses the image of God as birthing Mother and weeper. And at last Pastor Cheri breaks the silence, with the words, "Hannah, child of God, you have been sealed by the Holy Spirit and marked with the cross of Christ forever." The people nod. Grace approves. Grace agrees.

A Service Of Baptism

Leader: Baptism is the celebration of thanksgiving in the Christian community for the miracle and wonder of God's gifts of life. It is praise to God, the Creator and Sustainer of life, and wonder in each newborn child.

(Parents, infant [child], family, and close friends gather at the baptismal font.)

Parents: Because of God's love we bring this child to be baptized into this community of faith and love. We ask God's guidance in helping us to care for *(name of child).*

Leader *(to Parents)*: Will you therefore nurture *(child's name)* in the name of Christ, that by your teaching, prayer, and example *(he/she)* may grow and have life in His name?

Parents: I will.

Leader *(to congregation as Sponsors)*: Will you nurture and love *(child's name)* in the Christian faith and life?

Congregation: With God's help and empowered by the Holy Spirit we will proclaim the good news of God's love and live according to the words and actions of Christ our Lord.

Thanksgiving Over the Waters of Baptism:

Eternal Creator, in the beginning you birthed creation

As the Holy Spirit continues to birth creation in and through each of us,

While Your Word in Christ makes visible Your silence.

The Baptism
Leader: *(Child's name),* I baptize you in the name of God and of Christ and of the Holy Spirit.
All: Amen.
Leader: The Holy Spirit is at work within you, that being born of water and the Spirit you may be a faithful disciple of Jesus Christ.
All: Amen.

Commendation and Pledge
Leader: I commend to you *(child's name)* this day and ask if you will live so that *(he/she)* may grow in the knowledge and love of God?
Congregation: With God's help we so pledge. Amen.

Prayer:
All: Not in slavery but sonship
Not in despair but daughterhood
Not in fear but faith
We cry with Jesus, "Abba! Parent!" Amen.

TO DO WITH CHILDREN:
Read aloud the service of baptism to children before it happens so they will have time to ask questions or make comments.

Discuss the different kinds of baptism. If you do not practice immersion, visit a local Baptist church to acquaint children with the practice of believer's baptism. Contact the minister beforehand, asking him or her to show the baptistry, explain the ritual, and answer questions.

Visit your sanctuary when it is empty and ask the minister to explain and talk about the meaning and service of baptism. Discuss the differences between infant and believer's baptism.

Act out a baptism ceremony, role-playing the minister, parents, sponsors, and ushers, using a doll and a bowl of water as props.

Read and discuss the scripture references about baptism:
Jesus' baptism: Matthew 3:1-17
Jesus baptizing: John 3:22-26, and John 4:1-3

Jesus commanding his followers to baptism: Matthew 28:16-20

References to baptized person in the New Testament: Acts 2:1-11; Acts 8:13; Acts 8:26-40; Acts 9:1-20; Acts 10:1-48; Acts 16:11-15; Acts 18:8; Acts 19:1-7; 1 Corinthians 1:19-17.

---

1. C.S. Lewis, *The Voyage of the "Dawn Treader"* (New York: Collier Books, 1974), 89-91.

2. Richard Katz, "The Wisdom of Ancient Healers," *Sacred Stories,* ed. Charles and Anne Simpkinson (San Francisco: Harper, 1993).

3. Michael L. Lindvall, "A Child is Born" (*Good Housekeeping,* Dec. 1990), p. 116.

4. John D. Stoneking, "Saying Hello and Goodbye," *The Circuit Rider,* March, 1984, Nashville, TN.

5. Walter Wangerin, Jr., "Baby Hannah," *Miz Lil & the Chronicles of Grace* (San Francisco: Harper & Row, 1988).

14

The Sacrament Of Holy Communion

While they were eating, he took a loaf of bread, and after blessing it he broke it, gave it to them, and said, "Take; this is my body." Then he took the cup and after giving thanks he gave it to them, and all of them drank from it. He said to them, "This is my blood of the covenant, which is poured out for many (all). Truly I tell you, I will never again drink of the fruit of the vine until that day when I drink it new in the kingdom of God (Mark 14:22-25).

Communion has many meanings. It is the Lord's feast of liberation, the model for mutual sharing of justice and well-being. It is the messianic banquet where "all will be well and all will be well and all manner of things will be well." It is our memory of Jesus' last supper, and of the post-resurrection meal on the beach. It is God's gracious presence in the everyday elements of bread and wine.

In the sacrament of communion people do not eat bread to feed their bodies but to nourish their souls. We are hungry for so many things, and God knows that, and there is no limit to God's love or God's feeding. God feeds us with people we can love and touch and trust, with the Word of God we can hear and tell, and especially with the presence of Jesus in our midst, whom sometimes we even have the eyes to see.

As he said to his disciples, he says to us today, "Receive the Holy Spirit," the medium of divine love, pronounced in the sacrament to which we respond with justice and love.

It is believed that the institution narrative originally circulated as an independent narrative for the church's liturgical rite. The passion narrative contained no mention of the Last Supper; therefore it has important theological consequences, in that Mark regarded the Passover as a clue to the meaning of the Eucharist. Now it will be a memorial not to the Exodus, but to Jesus himself, a re-presentation (action) of God's deliverance and love.

Symbolic language and images are the creative work of the unconscious. They speak to imagination, emotion, and intuition. They point to transcendence, mystery that elicits our praise and thanksgiving, our petition, intercession, and confession of the heart. They speak as powerfully as words, for they speak to the senses as well as the unconscious. They are the poetry of words.

Sacraments are symbols that represent our relationship with God, the purpose and activity of worship. They make holy the sacredness of the ordinary, but though they are primary signs, God is always the ultimate. The sacrament of Communion is a ritual action that celebrates remembering and giving thanks, empowering us to work in the world.

The Eucharist celebrates the union of Jesus with humanity and with the earth, as it rejoices in the union of God with the universe in love and intimate communion with creation. God's word is our "bread," the bread we eat for our spirit's nourishment. God of the Hebrews was a God of the senses. Yahweh enjoyed the smell of meat sacrifice, used burning bushes from which to send messages, the mountain as a holy dwelling, and rode on the wings of the wind. The psalmist sang, "Taste and see the goodness of the Lord."

Sensing the Spirit we come to the sacrament of Holy Communion to feed the body and the spirit as one. As God is in God's word and Jesus in his words, the living Spirit of God is in our words, when we tell God's word and Jesus' stories. Jesus is the Incarnation of the Word that was with God from the beginning and we are God's stories, incarnations of God's Spirit.

We come as patients who go to a hospital because they are sick, as people who go to a table because they are hungry. We eat out of our need, not our worthiness. I sat in the back of the darkened church that night listening to a strange but exciting story of the death and resurrection of a man billions of people called God. Grateful for the dark, I glanced around the small, empty church. The woman my eyes rested on was sobbing and I identified with her,

176

for it was my own sad story that had brought me here. The sermon ended and we were invited to the altar to eat the bread and drink the wine. I had already fed on the word and again I was glad for the dark and did not move. This meal was not for me. I felt unworthy. I cried silently within my longing while I listened to the gentle sobs of the woman at the front of the deserted church. I saw the minister walk down the aisle and in an affectionate voice say, "Take, eat. It was meant for you, lassie." It was then I stood up to go forward for the food.

It was meant for all. The three-year-old, not wishing to be left alone in her pew, knelt beside her grandmother at the communion railing. When the minister passed her without offering her the bread or the drink, she turned to her grandmother and in a loud, puzzled whisper said, "But, Mumsie, I didn't get nothing."

Communion means a gathering, a coming together. As Christians we come to the same place, at the same time, each week on Sunday. We come because we gather to praise God, hear the sacred story, and join in Jesus' act of "breaking bread," eating together in his name. Bread is a symbol for Jesus, who said, "I am the bread of life."

The sacrament of communion is a sacrament of "belonging." The boy, sitting beside his father, reached to get the bread, and his father slapped his hand so hard he had to get up from the table because he was going to cry. Communion is a place where you can redefine your life, for at this table you can cry, you can laugh, you can enjoy.

Holy Communion is one of the rituals of the worshiping community that teaches without words. Children belong in the worship community. Children feel a sense of belonging when they are included through smiles, handshakes, Holy Communion, and stories. To belong is to be "tamed" by worship. In *The Little Prince*[1] the child is met by a fox. In order to be his friend, the fox explained, he must tame him and then told him how: "You must be very patient ... and you will say nothing. Words are the source of misunderstandings. But you will sit a little closer to me, every day ... One must observe the proper rites ..." "What is a rite?" asked the little prince. "They are what makes one day different from other days, one hour from other hours."

If worshiping God is the meaning of life, as Christians affirm, then children are included in the most important act in which their family participates. The Rev. Philip McLarty tells in *The Children, YES!* of his family's visiting his wife's home church at the time his children were six, four, and two. When the minister announced, "Please write your child's name on a card to receive a blessing as a substitute for taking communion," the six-year-old leaned over his brother to whisper to his father, "If I can't take it, you can't take it either." The father abstained.

John Calvin wrote, "As far as the Lord's Supper is concerned, I would rather experience it than understand it."

And Jesus, on the night he was betrayed, took bread, and when he had given thanks, he broke it and said, "This is my body, which is for you; do this in remembrance of me." The sacrament of Communion is that Love in which participants are united to each other and to God. It is an event to be experienced and remembered.

Because the sacrament of the Lord's Supper, the Eucharist, Holy Communion, celebrates our resurrected, living Lord, the worship of the early church was characterized by a sense of joy and thanksgiving (Acts 2:46-47). The way the Eucharist ("giving thanks") is celebrated forms and transforms the people's spirituality.

Because God fed the people in the wilderness and because Jesus shared his last meal before his death with his friends, early church worship occurred in the context of a meal. Jesus was known in the "breaking" of bread. He fed the multitudes, and after Jesus' death the disciples were grieving on the way to Emmaus. When the Stranger "took bread, gave thanks, broke it and began to give it to them" (Luke 24:30, Matthew 26:26), they knew who he was. In John Jesus met his friends on the shore of Galilee when "Jesus came, took the bread and gave it to them" (John 21:12-13).

Communion is a remembrance and an anticipation. It is a way of remembering and a promise of future meals, especially the Great Banquet where all will sit down at the table together and be fed.

Through the centuries the sacrament has become a sober one, recalling the gruesome death of Jesus' crucifixion. On the one hand a true cause for sadness. On the other hand a cause for celebration and joy in God's conquering the power of death. We, as post-resurrection Christians, can sing and dance, laugh and rejoice over the victory of the Lord of the Dance. The disciples left the last meal singing.

In the sacrament of Communion there is taking, blessing, breaking, giving, and receiving.

The Taking. Taking the bread means we are offered a choice: we may choose to take the bread or refuse. We may choose to receive the elements (reaching out for them) in the pew or standing up and coming forward to take the bread and cup. Taking requires choice and participation. The bread and wine are brought, presented, and offered. The church remembers herself as the body of Christ, and in the receiving of the Eucharist is the feeding and transforming of the body.

"Take, eat, and become the body of Christ in the world." In the taking we offer ourselves to God and one another. Jesus' people taught that whenever two people ate together, it symbolized, "You are my sister. You are my brother. I am responsible for you." The sober, serious German and Swiss tone of the Reformers, such as Luther and Calvin, however, emphasized the late medieval notion of the Eucharist as a sacrifice and dropped the "offering" of ourselves. Aware of the significance of Christ's death on the cross, they interpreted the atonement as blood sacrifice, the free grace of God's act and acceptance, thus undercutting the Jewish and modern understanding of faith as grace *and* work.

Action that lasts must have nourishment from the past, roots, or we will drift away from the influence of the past, and the action will lack roots. We have the "roots" in the story as tradition gives it to us. Its nourishment comes from remembering, for remembering opens the present to the creative power of the past. It is in the act of remembering that people establish their identity, their mission, and their meaning. As we gather each Sunday around our sacred stories to remember and reenact them, we become aware of who we are and whose we are. We know what we are to do. Jesus said, "Drink this cup in memory of me."

I said to the almond tree, "Tell me about God."

179

And the almond tree blossomed.

I said to Jesus, "Tell me about God."

And he broke the bread and said, "This is my body, given for you."

I attended the sneak preview of a film with a group of art critics. The film was *Places in the Heart*, a story of central Texas in the 1930s, with all the customs and prejudices that went with the time and place. It was a sophisticated audience. I was, therefore, unprepared for their reaction to the closing scene, where Holy Communion heals the brokenness of the leading characters. What surprised me was the absolute silence at the conclusion of the film — and then the thunderous roar of applause.

Communion is union and sharing, a partial realization of God's Promise for *all* people. It is the joyful feast of the People of God. "This is my body" is a cosmic body that includes all people, the entire universe in the living, risen, glorious body of Christ!

Communion is a sacrament for all human beings, for it is a ritual reminder that all of us depend on sharing resources in our global village. Jesus' last supper celebrated this sharing. We do not, therefore, take communion lightly. Are you willing to take the bread, which may mean sacrificing yourself for your sister or brother? Whenever that spirit exists between two or twenty or two thousand, the spirit of communion exists. So we are asked, "Will you take the bread?"

The Blessing. Jesus blessed the bread. To bless is to put a bit of yourself into something, to change something for someone because of your presence, to lean forward in love, being there for the other. The later liturgies of the church, which had become a church of many "words," included in the blessing introductory dialogue, preface, Sanctus, and thanks. Today individuals and some churches are recognizing the importance of silence, in contrast to a traditional wordiness. Jesus spoke in parables "to the point," pointing to God, and then he was silent. The church interpreted Jesus' words and even his silences so that our sanctuaries today are filled with words.

Again, the paradox of worship, the both/and, the balancing, silence complementing the words: God spoke through The Word and words, and God said, "Be still and know that I am God." Even before Pilate's question "What is truth?" Jesus was still.

The Reformers "tampered" with the words of the ancient blessing. Calvin dropped the entire section in favor of an exhortation after the words of institution. Aware that these ancient worship practices and words were models rather than Law, the Reformers interpreted them in the light of their theology. God lures us to new life in all forms (words and silences) inside and outside the church.

The Breaking. In Jewish practice breaking the bread was a way of making the bread available to the participants. In the course of Christian history it became symbolic of the breaking of Jesus' body on the cross. The term "breaking" refers to our condition as well.

Paul interpreted the one loaf as symbolic of the church's body (1 Corinthians 19:17). By the third century that unity was replaced by the symbol of Christ's broken body on behalf of the church.

Giving and Receiving. In the earliest liturgies the officiant gave the bread and cup to each individual, saying the words of Jesus or a paraphrase:

Officiant: The body of Christ, the bread of life.
Person: Amen.
Officiant: The blood of Christ, the cup of life.
Person: Amen.

Being fed, we go out to feed. When Jimmy Carter was President he invited Harry Haynes of the Methodist Committee on Overseas Relief to the White House. Haynes was curious as to the reason, and of course accepted the invitation. The president of Notre Dame was there as well. Carter did not keep his guests in suspense for long. He explained to them that he needed their help; he had discovered that Americans have the expertise and the food to feed the entire world for the next ten years but we need to change attitudes. The President needed their help.

Mark used the ritual meal of Passover with its story and symbols in order to tell his new story of the Human One who gave his life for all and we tell stories of the ritual meal that help us to "see" and feel.

Stories Of The Ritual Meal

1. A visitor was given a glimpse into heaven and into hell. His first visit was to hell. There he saw a magnificent banquet table filled with food. The people were dressed in rich and beautiful clothing but the people themselves were gnashing their teeth, and were all skin and bones, for the only implements they had to eat with were three-foot-long forks, which they were unable to get into their mouths. "Now let me see heaven," the man said to the angel. In heaven he saw the same magnificent banquet table filled with food and the same three-foot-long forks, but here the people were plump and jolly, for in heaven the people were feeding ... one another.

2. The Bag Lady stood before him, after he had opened to her knock on his door. She was different, however, from all the rest, for she had brought him a gift, the gift of a story. She told him of a village far, far away and long, long ago, in the center of which was a table and on the table was always a loaf of bread. Yet no one ever ate the bread, for there were stories that said if one took the bread, one could become a slave, or disappear, or even die. No one knew of any such person but they *remembered* the stories and that was all that mattered.

There was a ritual in that village that whenever girls or boys turned fourteen, they were brought to the table and asked, "Do you wish to eat the bread?" Always, out of fear, they said, "No." Three times they were asked and always the young person answered three times: "NO!"

One day a young boy turned fourteen and was brought to the table and asked, "Do you want to eat the bread?" He replied, "Yes." The people gasped, but they thought he had not heard the question. The elder asked again, "Will you take the bread?" "Yes." There was a long silence, giving the boy time to think about what he was saying, what he was doing. For the third time, the last time, the elder asked again, "Will you take the bread?" "Yes!" he said, and took the bread and ate.

He did not become a slave or disappear or die, but he did become a servant to all, and he did disappear for a while, but he returned to tell the people about a God who loved them so deeply that no matter what they would do, God would still love them. Some of the people were so disturbed by his stories that one day they killed him. Yet the word spread among the people that he still lived among them.

Then the Bag Lady got up from her chair and walked out the door. Her host followed her but could see no one, and when he returned, he saw that she had left her bag, and reaching within, he took out the *bread*, her second gift. *(Take bread from bag.)*

Soon you will be offered the bread, the gift of Christ among us, and you will have to decide whether or not you will take it, if you will die each day for another. But consider for a moment what life would be if no one ever took the bread. Then, having considered, decide and choose. "Will you, my beloved, take the bread?"[2]

3. An Italian couple getting married made arrangements with the parish priest to have a small reception in the parish courtyard outside the church. But it rained, and they couldn't have the reception, so they asked the priest if it would be all right if they had the celebration in the church. The Father was not happy about this, but they convinced him by saying, "We will eat a little cake, sing a little song, drink a little wine, and then go home." The Father agreed. But being good life-loving Italians they drank a little wine, sang a little song, then drank a little more wine, and sang some more songs, and within a half hour there was a great celebration going on in the church. And everybody was having a great time, lots of fun. All except the Father, who paced up and down in the sacristy, upset about the noise they were making. "I see you are quite tense," said the assistant pastor. "Of course I'm tense. Listen to all the noise they are making, and in the House of God, for heaven's sake!" "Well, Father, they really had no place to go." "I know that! But do they have to make all that racket?" "Well, we mustn't forget, must we, Father, that Jesus himself was once present at a wedding!" "I know Jesus Christ was present at a wedding banquet. YOU don't have to tell me Jesus Christ was present at a wedding banquet!" said the Father. "But they didn't have the Blessed Sacrament there!!!"[3]

To Do

Have an alternate service of communion.

The Service: (The week before this service, invite persons to bring food for sharing in response to receiving. Before the celebration of communion, however, be sure participants feel welcome to the celebration whether or not they have brought a gift for sharing.) "Some of you are visiting. Some did not hear of our bringing gifts of food to share at this feast and some have forgotten. You are welcome to this symbol of God's love with or without a gift. Please join with us."

The Story: On the night Jesus was betrayed he ate together with his disciples, celebrating the Passover, their memorial to the Exodus. Then Jesus took the bread and the cup, saying that it was now his body and blood, thus representing God's action of love.

The Invitation: This is the feast of the banquet of God who calls us to eat and drink and share what we have been given, in the name of Christ who shared his life in communion with humans in need.

The Acceptance of the Gift: We take this bread and wine in recognition of God's presence here and now.

The Response: We give thanks for God's love by leaving our gifts of food and drink at the altar as a symbol of our sharing God's banquet with all creation.

Have an "animal cracker communion" with younger children. Paul wrote in the Bible that he was a "fool for God." A friend of mine, serving animal crackers in the shape of a lion, would bite off a piece and meekly "meow," representing a kitten transformation, but when he ate the whole cracker, he roared. Made in the image of God, invited to the feast of celebration of Christ-with-us here and now, when we eat the bread and drink the wine, we too are transformed by the living Spirit among us.

Or, participate in a flower communion by gathering wildflowers before the service of worship. Place the flowers in several baskets (depending upon the size of the group) and pass them, asking each person to take a flower from the basket, present it to the person on their left, and affirm them by saying, "Bread and beauty are gifts of God. I offer you this gift in friendship in the name of Christ."

A friend of mine officiated her first sacrament of Holy Communion and found herself without bread. She had given it all away. There was no more. For the rest of the meal the senior pastor, while distributing the wine, said to each taker, "Pretend to eat. It will count."

The Sunday before Thanksgiving invite members to bring food gifts in recognition of the gift of receiving Communion.

Communion is a paradox, both in its meaning and its practice. The church has been called to live with diversity. An example is the decision whether to serve wine, alcohol that may cause the neighbor to "stumble," or grape juice, dangerous for the diabetic. Because of this some churches use intinction and choice. Participants come down the aisle to the altar area where they receive the bread and choose from either the wine on one side or the juice on the other in which to dip their bread.

After the concerns of the congregation are expressed aloud, conduct the Sacrament of Communion as a response to these concerns.

For Children

Bake bread or buy premixed bread in the grocery store and bake it. It is the smell and feel of the texture, as well as the taste, that is important for children to experience: 4 cups flour, 1 1/2 teaspoons yeast, 1 teaspoon salt, 1/4 cup oil. Dissolve yeast in 1/4 cup of warm water. Mix flour and salt. Add 1 1/2 cups of warm water, oil, and softened yeast. Knead until smooth. Cover with a damp cloth and let rise in a warm place for about 1 1/2 hours. Pinch off balls 1 1/2 inches in diameter and let rest under dry cloth for 30 minutes. Roll the balls 1/4-inch thick and 6 inches in diameter. Bake on ungreased sheet in preheated oven (350°) for 15 minutes. Broil one minute. Serve warm. Makes 18.

Make papier mache loaves of French bread as banks. Balloons are available in the shape of French loaves. Cut a slit in the top for money and allow to dry. When they are dry, paint and shellac them and use them for containers for the children's money offerings for hunger relief. To "take the bread" is to share with people who have no bread. Discuss the story by asking participants to complete the sentence: "The story said to me ..."

If you tell "The Bag Lady" to children, discuss the meaning of the Eucharist and "bag people." Have paper bags and explain that homeless people carry all of their belongings in a bag. "If you had to put all your possessions in one paper bag, decide what you would put in it."

Introduce a Communion hymn: The African-American spiritual "Let Us Break Bread Together" is based on Acts 2:42. The slaves used the third verse as a call for secretly meeting before sunrise for worship. In their native homes they used drums and horns as their call to worship. In this country their owners feared the power of these musical instruments to incite escape and rebellion. The first two stanzas were added after the Civil War and people began to use the hymn as an invitation to the Lord's Supper where all are welcome to gather and eat together.

In the Eucharist we sit down with Jesus in spirit and story, in body and faith imagination to fill our emptiness and empower our spirit.

---

1. Antoine de Saint Exupery, *The Little Prince* (New York: Harcourt Brace Jovanovich, 1971).

2. Based on a story by Joseph J. Juknialis, *When God Began in the Middle* (Saratoga, CA: Resource Publications, 1982), p. 44.

3. Anthony de Mello, *Awareness* (New York: Doubleday, 1990), pp. 65-66.

15

Children And Worship

When the church educates children, church teachers and leaders look for and participate in ways to involve them in worship.

Children learn through their senses and through storytelling. When the senses and the stories are united, there is participatory learning. Participatory learning lasts longer, is more fun, and is the most exciting and effective way to experience God.

The purpose of worship for children is to provide them a time and space to wonder, praise, and thank God. In so doing, the child may experience the presence of the Holy Spirit.

Worship is experience rather than explanation. Children learn through their feelings, their imaginations, and their experiences.

When we take seriously involving children in worship, all of the congregation benefits, for true religious education and worship feeds the emotions as well as the mind. Children experience before they understand, and as members of the church they have a place in church worship. They belong! Our Lord said and showed us so (Mark 10:13-16).

Children can become engaged in worship when the worship involves the whole person, the eyes in seeing, the ears in hearing, the nose in smelling, the body in movement from the simple lifting of the hands and arms in praise to God to the leap of joy in God's presence, as we read, "Pray everywhere, lifting up holy hands" (1 Timothy 2:8). Saint Augustine wrote that a Christian should be an Alleluia from head to feet.

The psalmist too knew the joy of using creative body movement as a means of better understanding our relationship with God, when he wrote, "Turn for me my mourning into dancing, that my soul may praise Thee" (30:11).

From time to time we adults need to be reminded that we have a "child" within us that needs to be fed and comforted, and that Jesus affirmed children, telling us to be "as children."

Families play a powerful and pervasive role in forming and feeding a child's faith life. The entire congregation is called the "family" of God. In this community children learn their sense of identity and sense of mission.

The family needs all the help it can receive from the extended church family as they bring up their children in the church. William H. Willimon, in "Keep Them In Their Place?" in *Worship Alive,*[1] told of the confusion and pros and cons over the issue of children and Sunday morning worship among the members of the Council on Ministries until a young mother spoke, almost with a tone of desperation in her voice, "I don't think some of you understand how difficult it is to raise Christians in today's world. We parents need all the help we can get. I feel that when my child's church gathers for worship, my child should be there."

There are specific ways in which we can invite children to worship. *Children and Worship*[2] suggests 62 activities, as well as listing reasons why children are included:

1. Children's time can be an important part of the act of worship in proclaiming, celebrating, and sharing the story. Children like stories that suggest and describe rather than lecture or present morals, that are full of action and meet children's need for hope and love and meaning. Use pictures, flannelgraph, and puppets to interest the children. Objects are helpful but not as "object lessons," because children do not understand abstract concepts. This is an important time to include children, not manipulate them.

Have objects of wonder, color, and beauty to be seen, such as flowers, shells, leaves, stones, fruits, pictures, colorful stoles, and stained-glass windows.

Stories from the Bible, such as John 5:1-9, can be told and the children asked to line them. Adapted stories from the Bible are available in books such as *Growing with the Bible, Old Testament Stories,* and *New Testament Stories,* available from Educational Ministries.

2. Invite the children to come forward for the reading of scripture so they can hear and see better. Give enough background for them to understand and a story that relates to the text.

3. Relate church school classes to what happens in worship, both in the area of the text to be preached and the content of the worship service.

4. Address children directly in the sermon without using gimmicks.

5. Underline key statements in the sermon manuscript, asking older children to write the gist of the idea in one sentence, and have them meet with the preacher afterward to review their answers.

6. Include children at the Lord's table, the mark of unity and fellowship in the body of Christ. Worship is to break the bread. It is the community's affirmation and praise of the Source of all life and love, naming the world in a particular way, based on Jesus' way of love. In worship we are fed. Worship is offering the water of baptism and the bread and wine of Holy Communion.

7. We do not restrict the meaning of Holy Communion to rational awareness. It is a gift of God's grace to be experienced. Invite the children beforehand to put on the tablecloth, fill the cup, bake or uncover the bread, help put things away after Communion. Some families may enjoy baking the bread on Saturday and bringing it to worship the next day.

8. Involve children in the learning and singing of hymns sung at the church worship, and practiced in choir or church school. Inviting them to choose new hymns and songs may enliven the service.

9. Older children can lead responsive readings, litanies, biblical skits based on the text for the day. Children can participate as banner or Bible bearers, acolytes, ushers, greeters.

10. Invite parents to plan with the worship leader or committee. Jesus said that unless we become as little children, we will not enter the realm of God. Brainstorm and write on the board the characteristics of little children.

Discuss: What are the rituals your church celebrates? What experiences of worship and prayer have your children had? What are their questions? What are your goals? What experiences can we plan to help them participate in worship?

---

1. William H. Willimon, "Keep Them In Their Place?" *Worship Alive!* (Nashville: Discipleship Resources).

2. Elaine M. Ward, *Children and Worship* (Prescott, AZ: Educational Ministries, 1993).

Bibliography

Recommended Reading

Carol Doran & Thomas H. Troeger, *Trouble at the Table, Gathering the Tribes for Worship* (Nashville: Abingdon, 1992).

Ruth C. Duck, *Finding Words for Worship* (Louisville: Westminster John Knox, 1995).

Cathy Townley, F. Michael Graham, *Come Celebrate! A Guide to Planning Contemporary Worship* (Nashville: Abingdon Press, 1995).

Elaine M. Ward, *Children and Worship* (Prescott, AZ: Educational Ministries, 1993).

Elaine M. Ward, *Love in a Lunchbox: Poems and Parables for Children's Worship*, (1996).

Robert E. Webber, *Signs of Wonder* (Nashville: Star Song Publishing Group, 1992).

Robert E. Webber, *Worship Old and New* (Grand Rapids, MI: Zondervan, 1994).

Ann Weems, *Reaching for Rainbows* (Philadelphia: The Westminster Press, 1980).

Bibliography for Creative Preaching

Frederick Buechner, *Telling the Truth: The Gospel As Tragedy, Comedy & Fairy Tale* (San Francisco: Harper & Row, 1977).

Anthony de Mello, *The Song of the Bird* (Garden City: Image Books, 1984).

Edward Hays, *Twelve and One-Half Keys, St. George and the Dragon, The Ethiopian Tattoo Shop* (Forest of Peace Books, Inc., Route One — Box 247, Easton, KS 66020).

Joseph J. Juknialis, *When God Began in the Middle* (San Jose: Resource Publications, 1982).

Eugene L. Lowry, *How to Preach a Parable: Designs for Narrative Sermons* (Nashville: Abingdon, 1989).

Eugene L. Lowry, *Doing Time in the Pulpit: Narrative and Preaching* (Nashville: Abingdon, 1985).

Charles L. Rice, *The Embodied Word (Preaching as Art and Liturgy)* (Minneapolis: Fortress, 1991).

Theophane the Monk, *Tales of a Magic Monastery* (New York: Crossroad, 1981).

Thomas Troeger, *The Parable of Ten Preachers* (Nashville: Abingdon, 1992).

Thomas H. Troeger, *Creating Fresh Images for Preaching* (Valley Forge: Judson, 1982).

Thomas H. Troeger, *Imagining a Sermon* (Nashville: Abingdon, 1990).

Walter Wangerin, Jr., *Ragman and Other Cries of Faith* (San Francisco: Harper & Row, 1984).

Paul Scott Wilson, *Imagination of the Heart, New Understandings in Preaching* (Nashville: Abingdon, 1988).